World Peace through True Love

FURTHER MESSAGES
IN THE
SPIRITUAL REALM
FROM
DR. SANG HUN LEE

HSA-UWC

Introduction

Dear Friends in Faith,

We are pleased to present to you at this time special revelations that can strengthen and edify your spirit and conviction in the power of God to transform this world. Throughout history mankind has searched for understanding concerning the purpose of life and the prophecies in scripture. Historically when God worked to guide His people, He would give revelation and inspiration through His messengers. When Abraham was about to offer Isaac, it was an angel that appeared and gave Abraham the message that God knew Abraham feared God in his heart and therefore his son did not have to be offered.

Herein lies an important lesson. When God reveals His messages to us, there is always an element of responsibility on humanity's part to believe in the message and the messenger. When Mary was told that she would bear the Christ child, the message was carried to her by the angel Gabriel. She believed in the message and in faith prepared and succeeded in giving birth to Jesus Christ, who would become the Messiah and Savior to humanity. Later when Jesus had matured and was in an hour of decision, God sent Moses and Elijah to him from the spiritual world to give him a message that gave insight into his mission and destiny.

We are honored to present to you messages from God, from the saints of all the major religions, and the former presidents of the United States. We also present confessions of repentance by former leaders of the communist world.

In II Corinthians 12:2-4, Paul writes, "I knew a man in Christ above 14 years ago, (whether in the body, I cannot tell; or whether out of the body, I cannot tell: God knoweth;) such a one caught up to the third heaven. And I knew such a man, (whether in the body or out of the body, I cannot tell; God knoweth;) How that he was caught up into paradise, and heard unspeakable words, which it is not lawful for a man to utter."

What are the unspeakable words that Paul heard? Believers

know that now we are living in times every bit as revelatory as that as the time of Paul, Jesus, Moses. Some may consider the textbook revealed from men and women either in the body or out of the body, and many would consider them unspeakable words. Like Paul, we know that there are believers who will understand God's message through these revelations. We humbly present them to you with sincere hope that they will enlighten you to the fact that the prophecy in the book of Acts 2:17, that in the last days God will pour our His spirit upon all flesh, is now being realized.

The Reverend Sun Myung Moon and Dr. Hak Ja Han Moon, True Parents of humanity, have made the family the cornerstone of their ministry. They teach that family is not restricted only to those who remain living with us, but also includes those who have passed on before us. The spiritual world is real. Understanding it can give the believer a more complete understanding of the purpose of life. It is with the heart of enhancing your whole life experience, both spiritual and that of this world, that we are presenting these revelations to you for your prayer and consideration. We sincerely hope they bring inspiration, hope and understanding in your journey toward heaven.

Sincerely, Rev. Michael Jenkins
President
Family Federation for World Peace and Unification, USA

Foreword

In his letter to the Hebrews, Saint Paul referred to this physical reality as a "copy and shadow" of the heavenly, or spiritual realm (Heb. 8:5). The Bible makes clear that life does not cease with the death of the flesh. Indeed, most major religions hold the concept that a person's soul continues on after his or her physical body passes away. Where the soul goes to dwell among the many mansions in the spirit world (John 14:2) is determined by the quality and character of his or her life on earth, especially the quality of faith and depth of love.

Up to the present, the realms of the spirit world have been divided, separated by the same barriers of religion, nationality, race and culture that divide people on earth. This is a natural consequence, as people on the other side continue with the same prejudices and limitations they had on Earth. However, in the Last Days, when God establishes His Kingdom, there should be unity in Heaven as well as on Earth, in order that "The Lord shall be one and His name be one" (Zech. 14:9) and "The kingdoms of this world become the kingdoms of our Lord and of His Christ, and He shall reign forever and ever" (Rev. 11:15).

The testimonies in these pages were uttered by leaders of diverse denominations and religions, even atheists, who gathered at special seminars in Heaven to study the truth of God and commit themselves to supporting the providence of this age. They have resolved to attend the one true God and Christ at the Second Advent. For some, it was their first experience of God's absolute and eternal love, and it shook them to their core. Others expressed profound remorse for their mistakes as well as gratitude for God's forgiveness. Through these testimonies, readers can see the process of the unification of Heaven unfolding before their eyes.

Today, many people are thirsty for knowledge about the heavenly world, and they seek out all manner of sources, some of dubious worth. A reliable source would be someone whom God has chosen to convey His message, for genuine prophecy "edifies the church" (1 Cor. 14:4). The Bible predicts that in the Last Days, "I will pour out My Spirit on all flesh, your sons and your daughters shall prophesy... and I will show wonders in the heavens and in the earth." (Acts 2:17-21). This indicates that the Spirit will inspire gifted individuals to have visions of the spirit world, showing people on Earth the wonders of Heaven. It also indicates that God's activity will encompass both realms. A study of the book of Zechariah, for instance, shows that prophets sometimes worked with heavenly spirits to better grasp the meaning of their revelations.

To convey these testimonies of the latter-day reorganization of Heaven and Hell, God has chosen two individuals, one to work in Heaven and the other to report about this work to people on the Earth. Dr. Sang Hun Lee was born in Korea in 1914 and passed into the spirit world at age 84. He is best known for his incisive critique of Communism, which was widely disseminated around the world during the Cold War era, and for his philosophical systematization of the Divine Principle, Rev. Moon's teaching. Zealous to unite all religions and philosophies by elevating them with this newest expression of God's truth, Dr. Lee had countless experiences teaching atheists and believers of various religions.

After passing into the spirit world, Dr. Lee continued to work tirelessly as a teacher. God allowed him to meet and interview some of the most notable figures in history, saints and sinners, from Jesus, Buddha and Muhammad to Stalin and Hitler. For his tireless efforts and devotion, God calls him "a man of the Heavenly Kingdom" and gave him the mission to educate all spirits. Specifically, Dr. Lee organized and led the seminars at which the testimonies recorded in these pages were given.

Dr. Lee's earthly counterpart is Young Soon Kim, an elder in the Unification Church who is graced with the gifts of spiritual hearing and spiritual sight. While in the Spirit she was able to hear Dr. Lee's interviews with the people at the seminars and record them on paper for earthly people to read.

Knowing that this information is new and unusual to many readers, we encourage you to digest it with a prayerful yet open mind. Heaven's use of terminology is sometimes different from its meaning on Earth. The term "Messiah," for example, as used throughout the narrative should be understood broadly.

When Jesus was accused of making himself God in John 10:33-35, he answered by quoting Psalm 82: "I said, You are gods, and all of you are children of the Most High," comparing his divinity to that which all are meant to inherit. Thus the anointing or Messiahship used here in reference to Rev. Moon does not mean that the revelations claim that Rev. Moon is Jesus. Jesus' role as Savior and Messiah will never change. What it does indicate is that Jesus anointed Rev. and Mrs. Moon as the True Parents of humanity to complete the work of the Second Advent by establishing true families as God's dwelling places. As Jesus predicted: "He who believes in Me, the works that I do he will do also; and greater works than these he will do" (John 14:12).

The book of Hebrews describes the Old Testament saints as a "cloud of witnesses" surrounding and urging on Christians as they run their race, on the principle that those saints in Heaven "should not be made perfect apart from us" on the Earth (Heb. 11:39-12:1). In the same way the saints are calling out to us today, describing to us the current situation from the vantage point of Heaven. They are urging us to do our part, so that together we might see the dawning of the Kingdom of God.

The saints who testify in these pages are united in their determination that "God's will be done on earth as it is in heaven." They bear witness that the Reverend and Mrs. Sun Myung Moon are fulfilling this mission on the Earth today. We encourage the reader to move beyond these messages and duly pursue study of their teachings and works. Those of us who have followed their leadership confirm the testimonies of the saints. We believe in God's work for world peace, to bring His kingdom upon the earth and in Heaven. With that love and hope in our hearts, we recommend these messages to you.

The Editors

A Letter From God

December 28, 2001

Dear beloved True Parents,

I am God, the Creator of the universe and the God of all humankind.

My beloved son! My son, I love you greatly! I hold you dearly! You are My pride and joy! My happiness and gratitude for you is limitless. I would search the cosmos to find the word that would fittingly describe My love for you, but I cannot find it. Mere words cannot adequately express My heart.

Because you, the True Parents, have succeeded in raising up everything that had fallen and restoring it to its proper status, I proclaim that you are truly the Savior, Messiah, and King of Kings of all humankind!

On December 25, 2001, the founders and leading figures of Christianity and the other major religions adopted a written resolution in which they all without exception resolved to participate in My providence for the peaceful unification of the cosmos. They resolved to attend the True Parents, who are in charge of this providential effort. Therefore, it is right and proper that the True Parents be exalted as the True Parents of all humankind.

I, the God of all humankind, invite you to ascend to the position of King of Kings. This position must be fulfilled internally, even though earthly people do not yet fully understand. You took up My cross and endured countless difficulties in My stead. Therefore, now I want to bestow upon you all My inspiration, gratitude, enthusiasm and ecstatic joy. Now I want you to inherit everything that is Mine.

True Parents, I want to embrace you in My bosom and never let you go! I would hold you all night long, and we could speak intimately as lovers do.

I am the God of all humanity, yet many centuries passed since I last knew a person on the Earth whom I could completely trust. I know and remember all the difficulties, pain and suffering that you endured for My sake. I experienced it all with you. Those crosses were all My responsibility, yet you carried them and endured, and now you have raised a victorious standard. Thank you, thank you, True Parents! Thank you for your dedication and hard work! Thank you for your victory, which has eased the pain in my heart and illuminated the cosmos! My gratitude will remain forever.

Victory to my beloved True Parents!
Victory to the Saviors of humanity!
Victory to the King of Kings!
Sincerely,
The God of All Humankind

Messages from the Principals
at the Seminar

1. Jesus' Message to Christians and All People on Earth

Jesus is using this opportunity to send this new message to people on Earth, including the Jews who are still waiting for the coming of the Messiah. Whether Christian or non-Christian, people know my name, Jesus.

The heart of Jesus who is sending this message to the Earth is complex and perplexing. I feel sad that I cannot summarize and convey my message in a few words. In particular, I know that Christians will doubt the message rather than believe it. However, as a person who came to the Earth with the mission of saving the world as the Messiah in the New Testament Age, since the time to reveal the truth has arrived, I am telling you the truth before Heaven and Earth.

I came to Earth with the mission from God to be the Messiah. In the Bible I could not reveal all of the conflicts between the religious believers and non-believers in those days. In fact, there are many providential matters that the Bible does not reveal. With the flow of each providential age, God could not avoid changing His immediate plan. I am revealing clearly a part of this hidden providential content to the numerous clergy who have been waiting for the Lord's return.

God created human beings to need a physical body during their earthly life. Once they lose it, they go to the spirit world and live there for eternity. Dear saints who are waiting for my return, why don't you pay attention to the fact that God gives dual prophecies in the Bible [blessings for those who follow His will, curses for those who disobey His will]? I came to Earth as the Messiah in the New Testament Age. What do you think is the meaning of the crucifixion? Do you really think that it was God's will from the beginning, or could it have been the result of human error? Have you thoroughly studied my life? I certainly came with the mission of the Messiah, yet I lived eating and sleeping like any other man on Earth. Even though I lived as an ordinary human being, my mission as the Messiah was unique. To state the conclusion, the way of redemption through my crucifixion was not God's original intention.

Dear Christians and all people on Earth, please pray over this matter while fasting. Then I will appear to you and clearly tell you the truth. When you do it, you should be totally focused on praying with a pure heart. Reverend Sun Myung Moon is the one who came to Earth to complete my mission that was not fulfilled through the redemption of the cross. He comes as the True Parent to conclude God's providence in the Completed Testament Age.

I came with the mission of the Messiah in the New Testament Age, but people at that time crucified me. That is why there remained a task for God to fulfill, and the necessity of a Second Coming. The Messiah in the New Testament Age brought salvation to people in the spirit. Still, history continued with the homework of physical salvation remaining to be fulfilled. Wandering in the alleys of grievance, suffering, sorrow and pain, God endured endless tension and pressure while He waited to send the Messiah again to Earth. After separating good and evil in order to prepare his lineage, God could send Reverend Sun Myung Moon.

You know where I was born; it was in a manger. Do you know what the heart of Mary was like at that moment? Dear fellow Christians, could you easily understand it from reading the Bible? Have you not struggled over some incomprehensible events or insoluble questions? How could you understand my heart, when I could not fully reveal all the secrets of heaven? How could you understand the intricacies of the providence, when so much was not recorded in the Bible? Why was the womb of Mary, Joseph's fiancée, growing large? You cannot understand all the secrets that have been veiled during the providence of restoration. Since human beings are children of God, God cannot help but love them. It is also difficult for you to fathom the heart of God.

Reverend Sun Myung Moon is the returning Messiah for whom you have been waiting and waiting. He inherited my mission at the age of 16. Dear Christians, are you still looking up and waiting for Christ to return on the clouds? Reverend Moon travels throughout the world on the clouds. He is investing all of his heart and soul for the realization of world peace. Even today, although he is over 80 years old, he is fighting on the frontline.

Are you going to hang him on the cross again, like the Romans who persecuted me 2,000 years ago? Aren't you aware of the destruction of Sodom and Gomorrah? God is love. He is waiting. Please receive the Messiah who has descended in the Completed Testament Age. Do not reject his achievements and his dispensation for the salvation of humanity. Pray with sincerity. I, Jesus, will be with you in your earnest prayers.

I sincerely wish that Christians would reflect deeply upon the circumstances when I, the Messiah of the New Testament Age, was crucified. I hope they pray about my life and about God's view on human salvation.

Think about the circumstances that I could not be married even though I was 33. Think of how my 12 disciples and I often went hungry. My life was filled with grievances. Christians surmise that everything that happened to me was the will of God. However, think whether there was any responsibility on the part of human beings. I came as the Messiah and the Son of Man. As the begotten Son of God, I did my very best to fulfill my messianic mission, but I could not fully accomplish my dreams and desires. Had my will been entirely fulfilled, would it be necessary for me to return?

Dear fellow Christians and religious believers, I am truly the Messiah. However, the one who returned to fulfill the messianic mission today is Reverend Sun Myung Moon. He is the Second Advent of the Lord. Think of the question John the Baptist asked me, when I was being hounded as a ringleader of heretics: "Are you the one who is to come?" How do you now see Reverend Moon? Think of the flow of time and examine the incredible achievements he has wrought. Could he do this by human power and ability alone?

Jesus who died physically cannot come back to physical life and appear to you. Human flesh is to return to the earth as dust, once it gives up the spirit. That is the truth and a heavenly law. Read again the Bible verse that states that people will rise from the tombs. God is the Author of science and mathematics as the Being of the Principle. The theory that a dead body that decomposed will be reassembled and float in the air assumes that God can do anything and everything. However, to have God violate His own Being is extremely contradictory! You cannot solve questions that way. Look at the world of nature. Look at the process of human growth and the design of human life. God and human beings are in a relationship of parent and child. You will have to experience the heart of God now, who has been leading the providence of salvation for humankind so patiently. What if you Christians could see me right now, sitting and talking with Buddha, whom you consider to be an idol worshipper? What would you think of me?

Dear fellow Christians, fellow Buddhists, and believers of various religions! The four great religious founders, Jesus, Buddha, Confucius, and Mohammed, and saints such as Socrates, Augustine and others, have already held this seminar a number of times. Its theme is always the same: "God is the Parent of All Humankind." During the seminars, we are always studying the Divine Principle revealed by Reverend Moon. We analyze and discuss it in depth.

That is the homework given us by God, who carefully observes all the activities of Reverend Moon on Earth. God has also directed that the major religious leaders in the spirit world unite and cooperate with earthly people for the salvation of humankind.

We religious founders have no barriers among us. We are united as one, through the Messiah who appears on Earth in the Completed Testament Age and gives rebirth to all humankind as the children of God. We are praying about and discussing how to create one world centered on God. The conflicts and confrontations often seen among religious people are resolved here in the spirit world. It took a long time for this to happen, to persuade people to understand one ultimate truth: the Creator of human beings is God alone. Likewise, in order to bring peace on Earth, it will be necessary to break down the barriers among all religions on Earth.

Earthly leaders of each religion should discuss the common-alities and differences among their different faiths. Together they should choose the strongest points from each, while showing the virtue of humility before others. Would non-believers not be guided in the right direction by following their example? I hope that all religious followers, especially Christians, can unite as one, and that I can meet them all in one place.

The fact that Jesus from Bethlehem in Judea could send a message to earthly people is due to the benefit of the age wrought with the arrival of the Completed Testament Age. Reverend Sun Myung Moon is the master of this era because he is the Messiah of the Second Coming.

What will you do with him? Are you going to put him on the stand for judgment? Are you going to hang him, as I was hung 2,000 years ago? Are you willing to pray and fast about this? I hope that you will make a wise decision as a religious follower. I send this message to earthly people with a desire to teach people about my responsibility as Jesus, the Messiah of the New Testament Age.

April 5, 2001

2. The Buddha's Message to Buddhists and Believers in Other Religions

I would like to send a last message to religious people on Earth, especially to Buddhists. As was mentioned by Jesus, as the representatives of each major religion, we four religious founders are making efforts for world peace and the salvation of humankind. This may not be comprehensible to earthly people. In the spirit world, the four major religious founders and other saints and sages are often gathered together for seminars, where we have no confrontations or conflicts with each other.

Before coming to the seminars, we were individually educated in the Divine Principle and other subjects, having attended several workshops. Was it easy to create such a gathering of the founders of religions? It was possible only after many prayers and special conditions, with thorough and repeated reviews and analysis. Now through these seminars, we can discuss things as members of the same family. We have no conflicts based on religious prejudices. Whenever we are gathered for this purpose, God embraces us with a splendid light and slowly leaves us in a friendly atmosphere, joyfully looking at us.

Dear Buddhists, even Jesus testified that he came with a messianic mission in the New Testament Age. What I did was similar. According to the Bible, the Completed Testament Age is to arrive after the Old Testament Age and the New Testament Age. Whenever a certain providential period arrived, God led a new dispensation through a new central figure.

Although my path as the Buddha was not in the mainstream of God's providence, it is undeniable that I strove to guide people to goodness. Further, I believe that encouraging Buddhists to keep their celibacy while waiting for the right time to arrive was quite effective for their spiritual training and cultivation, even if it was not the direct way to God. From the perspective of Christian history, the time of the Buddha was like the Old Testament Age. It may be unfamiliar, but during that time the benefit of the age for human salvation could not go any further. Buddha lived on earth during that time period, and his teachings were quite influential.

Dear Buddhists, I am not saying that your way of life thus far has been wrong. Like Jesus, in my time I also did my best to guide humankind in the right direction. However, with the passing of time, the tasks needed for the salvation of humankind have changed. What I am trying to do is to engraft the fruit of Buddhists who were raised through my methods of spiritual cultivation. Please study the Unification Principle. You will find there a considerable number of truths that also flow through the teachings of Buddhism. Do not be immersed in old-fashioned ideas and concepts, but by accepting the new truth, engraft it to the truth of Buddhism. Then I am sure that a wonderful passage of faith will open to you.

In this age Reverend Sun Myung Moon is the Buddha for whom you have been waiting. Make a special condition as a Buddhist at a shrine. It is time for you to be true to the highest standard of Buddhist integrity. Do not reject the new Buddha, who is to come in the Completed Testament Age. Do not reject his truth.

Demonstrate the virtue of compassion as practiced by numerous Buddhists who have cultivated their spirituality. Do not look for faults in others, but act with humility and prudence. What is truth? Depending on the historical era, the direction for human beings can change. Look at the world of nature. All things God created can change in color and size, depending on the environment, but the species remain the same. Who can quell the voice of the original mind, through which human beings are striving to lead a life of faith? However, depending on the sound of the voice of the original mind, the mode of human life can vary, bringing different aspects of joy to God.

Therefore, do not be fixed on an old-fashioned idea. Expand the horizon of your ideas and views. If I told you Jesus and Buddha are getting along as brothers, you Buddhists would not believe me. However, I cannot help it. God wants us to work together as one. In your opinion, what would Jesus call Buddha? He calls him "Honored Buddha" with a smile and a soft voice, always being humble. Once Buddha speaks, he always responds positively, with a bright and cheerful expression, saying: "Yes, right," "That is correct," and "Let's do it."

Dear fellow Buddhists and Christians, as Heaven and Earth are united as one, bringing the world of peace, should the Earth not be united as well? Let us be unified by the new truth in this new era. Reverend Sun Myung Moon is leading the Completed Testament Age, and he is the Buddha to come. This is the conclusion drawn in these seminars of the four major religious founders. Let us now liberate God, by bringing oneness between Buddhism and Christianity.

April 6, 2001

3. Confucius' Message to Confucianists and All People on Earth

When human beings live in the flesh, in order to sustain their physical life they decide on certain norms and live within that boundary. Human beings did not know better, being limited by their physical senses. They tried to cope with problems within limited boundaries, by seeing and hearing what appeared to be reality. Although the four major religious founders thoroughly reveal the contents they learned in these seminars, since they are invisible to the eyes of earthly people, people of earth cannot readily accept it as real.

However, the four major religious founders and other saints and sages here struggled more than anyone else for the salvation of humankind. Other than Jesus they may not be messiahs, but they willingly denied their physical comfort for the sake of humanity. Never taking life lightly, they are the ones who proclaimed the truth and sought to teach it to people, guiding them to a better life. Such are the individuals gathered together here.

Even after they offered their physical body, they cared for and cherished their followers on Earth as themselves. Because they endeavored and toiled so hard to guide them to a better direction, they are qualified to attend these gatherings.

As was already stated by Jesus and Buddha, the spirit world here is truly harmonious. Jesus introduced himself before the Buddhist participants and said: "Since we are gathered together, let us have worship in both the Christian way and the Buddhist way. And let us talk about our views on the life of faith." Likewise, Buddha offered a full bow to the Christians at the gathering and humbly said, "Thank you for giving me a chance to greet you." These two great founders then exhorted everyone to reconcile with each other despite some differences in their beliefs. Then some noise arose from a corner of that gathering. Jesus said in a gentle voice: "Dear brothers and sisters, we all are children of God and therefore brothers and sisters to each other. And it is time for us to show God harmony among us." The atmosphere calmed down and turned solemn. Then, God appeared as light. He swirled quietly in the beginning and later transformed the entire area into brightness. Everyone there was taken aback with surprise and mesmerized by its splendor. They did not know what to do.

During our seminars, God frequently demonstrated His thoughtfulness. I believe that such meetings will continue. We believe that through gatherings among the four great religious founders and other saints and sages, all power struggles among religions and denominations will disappear. Then the doors to the truth will open to all people from different backgrounds.

Dear Confucianists, how can I help you? In the world there are various races, religions, cultural backgrounds and customs that change depending on the situation. Despite that, all people have one thing in common: our human identity. Regardless of whether we are white, black, or yellow, once a person goes to a hospital, the method of treatment is identical for the same ailment. It is so because the human anatomic structure does not vary with race.

What does this mean? It means that we all have the same Creator. There is only one Creator, who is God. God is our Parent. If we attend Him, all will be well.

Nevertheless, why is everything so complicated? Ever since the wrong beginning of human history, different religions have arisen. The unification of religions is therefore necessary, and for this purpose God sent Reverend Sun Myung Moon to the Earth. He does not say that the religious doctrines taught by each religion are wrong, but presents one simple truth that everyone can unite with. Yet each religion still insists that their teaching alone is correct and the only right way. That is why things became so complicated. So I believe that we desperately need to yield to each other with a willingness to accept others. No matter how noisy it is on Earth, the representatives from the major religions are tightly bonded here. Bonded by what? There is only one truth. All of us have resolved that we will live with God, attending Him as our Parent. What then will my followers on Earth do? It is not difficult to guess.

Dear Buddhists! Your greatest teacher is attending God as the Parent of all humankind. God is your great Maitreya Buddha. Thus, you should no longer dwell in self-centeredness, but instead, examining your daily life on Earth, live in preparation for your future life here in the spirit world.

Humankind is one people and one tribe. Reverend Sun Myung Moon was sent to attend only one God and teach His heavenly law. Find out what he is doing for human liberation, despite the fact that he is over 80.

Dear earthly people! The place you will dwell for eternity is here in the spirit world. Earthly life is nothing but a temporary training center. During the harvest time, only good grain will be stored. Thus you should live a mature life. Dear followers of Confucius, please consult the messages from Jesus, Buddha, Confucius, and other saints and sages, and make a wise decision for your future life.

April 7, 2001

4. Mohammad's Message for Muslims and People on Earth

When God created human beings, each individual was to be an object of joy to Him. However, against His original will, due to the fall of the first human ancestors, from the beginning human history flowed in a wrong direction. Races divided, religions arose, and different cultures developed depending on the living environment. Nevertheless, the Creator of all human beings is only one, God. How painful His heart must be when He looks at the divisions of humankind into many races, religions and cultures. God is the Parent of all humanity, but when He has to watch His children fighting every day, arguing over who is right and who is wrong, how must He feel? Earthly people do not know the overall direction and flow of God's providence, nor the relationship between God and human beings, and that is why there has been no harmony among religions for a long time.

God is the Parent of humanity. If examined carefully, the original source of all doctrine or truth is one. What religion would teach people to revere evil? Although their methods might differ, their fundamental purpose is to pursue goodness. God is the original being of absolute goodness and love, and every religion teaches about love.

Therefore, the fundamental teachings of each religion are quite similar. Now God's basic desires are to bring the truths and doctrines of all religions together and unite them as one. When it is done, God can finally rest. After countless days of waiting, God finally sent Reverend Sun Myung Moon for this purpose. Through him, the Unification Principle was revealed for the sake of the unification of all religions.

Dear Muslims, you too were born as children of God. I hope that you will unite in one thought. The reason is simple. The only God wants that unification. God at the time of Mohammad and God in this era is the same God, who is our unchanging Parent. Now is the time when we should be able to enjoy one brotherhood and realize world peace. God desires it all the time.

The possibility of world peace is remote without the unification of religions. Dear Muslims, Mohammad is petitioning you. Do not employ our own unique faith and doctrines to cause pain to other religious believers, but accept everyone with open arms and open hearts. By so doing, open doors to conversations on doctrines and join together. The four major religious founders have united in one thought and idea. Jesus accepted Buddha, and vice-versa. We personally experienced God who is rejoicing to see us at the same seminar. Through that experience, we resolved to remain united as one.

Reverend Sun Myung Moon came to the Earth in order to deliver God's will and to unite a divided and scattered humankind. He appears as the True Parent. I hope that my followers will also accept him with a humble attitude.

The one whom you have been attending is God. When you work with other religious believers after accepting God's love, both God and Mohammad will praise you.

And please read thoroughly the Unification Principle in a quiet place. Mohammad opened his heart all the way, after realizing from the seminar that its teaching is a true guide to human life. I know that you cannot do it overnight. However, if it is a path that everyone must go, I hope that none of you will fail in choosing the right and straightest way for your life.

April 9, 2001

5. Message of Socrates to Intellectuals

After the senators in Athens betrayed me, I often thought that it would have been nice if human life could have been valued and cherished more than my theories that so disturbed the citizens. Human life should not be judged by what is visible. Even the smallest creature was created with the loving care of God's hands. If so, how precious and valuable human beings must be as children created with all of God's heart and soul, the masterpieces of all creation!

Although created as children of God, human beings have lived without knowing it. Think of the relationship between parents and children on Earth. When they are apart from each other, how much do they long with aching hearts to see each other? Parents and children should live in happiness, sharing love and conversation in the same family. Even God desires to live like that. God, the Creator of human beings, is the original source of love and heart itself. Yet since the creation, due to the wrong direction the first human ancestors took, the relationship between God and human beings has been severed. Under those circumstances, what has been the heart of God?

You know Socrates is a man who was betrayed by the jury in Athens. The pain and sorrow that I experienced from that injustice was indescribable. After coming to God, however, I discovered Someone who was mistreated more than me, bearing more chagrin and grievances. It is because human beings did not know their relationship with God. What could be more grievous, lamentable and unfair? Human beings have not known their own Parent, nor the love by which He has been dearly caring for them, nor the pain He has had to endure for so long as He waited for His children to return. When I realized this, my sorrow was beyond words.

Dear intellectuals! Between parents and children, is there boasting about knowledge and academic position? The most important thing to us is to restore and maintain the parent and child relationship. Its value is greater than the discovery of any academic theories. Would Socrates not know how important it is for human beings, especially intellectuals, to have a position in worldly society? Regardless, remember that attending your Parent well is so important. In fact, it cannot be compared with anything else. What else could be needed other than God? When we say, "God is my Parent and I am His child," it means that the relationship bonded in blood lineage bestows the greatest position.

Dear intellectuals! Physical bodies are required only during earthly life. So it is with your knowledge and academic position. Therefore, even in preparing to register here for your future life, you need to be equipped with inner knowledge. Being so ignorant, while intoxicated by your academic skill, if you suddenly separate from your flesh body, where will your spirit go? This is a serious matter to consider. Remember that another world definitely exists, and your spirit will live there for eternity.

Accordingly, unprepared spirits cannot stay here. Have you ever seen beggars on the street? Lacking their own home, they stay anywhere on the streets. Likewise, you should prepare your haven in the spirit world. External knowledge and academic status were important to me during my earthly life, but more than these I pursued human beings' inner spiritual life and the truth of philosophy.

You cannot imagine how much time I invested for this. Since I unceasingly sought human beings' inner truth, not the momentary life on earth, I was granted this position as the representative of all intellectuals and people who prize reason above all. How can there not be awards given for the conscious endeavors one makes to come to the eternal world? The fruit of your hard work, effort and investment is borne here, in the dwelling place of eternal happiness.

I had to pass numerous tests before I could send this message. What were they? Here in this world as on Earth, people have various ways of life. As on Earth there are also many different religious entities. One day I attended a seminar for intellectuals, during which I listened to a lecture on the Divine Principle with the theme: "The Path for Intellectuals to Go." I encountered a new truth, one that was awakening me to the fundamentals of life. Yet since I was being transformed into a new person so drastically, my pride was hurt. Many times I shook my head, trying to deny the new truth that I was hearing. I also hoped that it was not true. Then, when I discovered from where such an incredible truth originated, conflicts and friction arose in my heart. I was ashamed of myself, for I felt my dignity and authority as an intellectual were being totally stripped away. However, what can I do about the truth? Truth is truth no matter what. After realizing this, I gave up on my intellect and pride. I decided to invest everything into this truth. I had to pass that test before I came to send this message to intellectuals on Earth.

Dear intellectuals! Even if I were to mobilize all of my intelligence and reason, how would it compare with that of God? Would God have created all things randomly, without any plan? Even if I could sell my intelligence and abilities, I could not purchase those belonging to God. No matter how great the power of science, can natural law be changed? God Himself is the Master of science. The mightiness and divinity of God that Socrates discovered cannot be described in words.

That is not all. The lady who is taking down my message is an earthly person, but I am a spirit dwelling in the spirit world. Can you intellectuals understand this? Such communication is also possible only due to the power and ability of God. Since the time is ripe, God is allowing me to reveal heavenly secrets to earthly people so that they can be guided to the right place in the future.

Here in the spirit world, resolution of difficulties comes simply because people here have already verified and understood the situation of God. Their directions are also the same, consistent with that of God. However, on Earth things are very complicated, simply because there is no agreement on what is the right direction.

Dear intellectuals! God is toiling hard to guide His children in the right direction, mobilizing various methods. Ladies and gentlemen, have you ever seen God? He is invisible and formless. Nevertheless, His single-minded desire to restore His lost children is unchanging even after many thousands of years. That is why He sent Reverend Sun Myung Moon to Earth on His behalf, and presented us with the Divine Principle. He wants us to determine the right direction to take in our lifetime. The book *Exposition of the Divine Principle* was not written by a human brain or deduced by human reason. It is a book of salvation that was discovered through Reverend Moon's bloody battles against Satan. He verified every single thing in the book as truth from God. It contains everything. Read it carefully. Your intellect is able to analyze how much your spirit is awakened, and you will be able to realize the direction you should take in your life.

Dear intellectuals! Who are the people whom you should most highly respect as great? Ask and answer that question yourself. They will very likely be people who left behind something valuable on Earth. Yet so far, there have not been great people who willingly took responsibility for the next life in the spirit world. Reverend Sun Myung Moon, on behalf of God, is guiding us toward an eternal passage to peace. Through his mission he awakens our spirit. Then he is willing to be responsible for our life in the next world.

Study him and try to find teachers greater than he, comparing them. If you cannot find any earthly persons who are greater than he, what will you do? You are in a serious position at a serious time, and you are required to make a serious decision in your life. Life is not long, but the next world absolutely exists. Don't you think that it is wise for you to meet a true teacher and be prepared for the next life, by studying what he teaches?

God does not need your knowledge or intelligence. Only humble people can be with God. By learning His great and profound truth and digesting it as your own, you should be able to be more than a beggar when you come to this world in the future. The highest intellectuals should be among those who can attend God as their Parent. In fact, only such individuals can be considered the highest intellectuals.

April 10, 2001

Communist Thinkers

1. **Karl Marx** (1818-1883, the founder of Marxism; born of a Jewish family in Trier, Germany.)

"God exists as Parent of humankind."

I attended here to confirm that I, Marx, affirm God's existence and that He is the Parent of all humankind. I denied God and shouted loudly with confidence to the extent that people believed me more than God. Now I'd like to reveal my experience with God to the whole world.

I met Dr. Lee for the first time in the spirit world and was very attracted by having several talks about theory with him. I felt that my theoretical paradigm was crumbling as I listened to his Godism lecture. At the same time my pride was damaged severely. When I listened to Godism, I thought it was a dream, but it was not. Then a beam of light came into my heart like a red-hot bullet. After moving through the air with the light, I came to see a miserable scene. I thought it likely that I was in Hell. Then I heard a voice saying, "Look at that. The poor children of God are groaning here. Save them. Be responsible for them. God is the Parent of all human beings."

My whole body was covered with sweat, as if it had been raining. I saw a very miserable scene. My chest was choking and I was in such pain that I couldn't stand it. I told Dr. Lee what I experienced. Dr. Lee said, "That's your responsibility. Think it over." After my experience of God's light, I have felt God always with me. Dr. Lee opened a new theoretical perspective to me.

All the thinkers in this cosmos! I, Marx, have met God. I have found that He is the Parent of humankind. I have felt the greatness of God's love. I clearly convey to you who God is. He is the Parent of humankind. Reverend Sun Myung Moon, who is on the Earth, brought this fact to light. The *Divine Principle* and *Unification Thought* express the original standards that open the way to salvation, so you must read them. I ask this of you seriously. I clearly say that I apologize for my past to God and True Parents and I love them and am proud of them. Marx, 4.18.2002

2. **Friedrich Engels**
(1820-1895, Marx's lifelong fellow thinker.)

"The Divine Principle *saved me."*

When I look at the harmonized cosmos and the organization of human beings, I have no excuse for my past years of denying God. I expect my example to become a lesson for the people on Earth and in the spirit world. And I want to tell you the impression I have from the *Divine Principle* education. I would like to clearly and honestly point out the way humankind must go. Don't believe in other gods, but place your hope in God.

Because of my strong pride, I neglected God when I was on the Earth. I could see nothing but actual beings and thought that those who believe in God are weak people. I spent my life on the Earth without knowing that life on Earth is very short. I, who denied God and spirits, was very miserable when I came to the spirit world. I doubted that life here was connected with that on the Earth, even after I lived here. How can I express even a part of my bitter heart? I have no way to deny that I, who denied God and this world when I was on the Earth, now live in the spirit world.

People on Earth, please listen to my confession. There were many questions about life in the spirit world that I couldn't answer. But after I learned the *Divine Principle* and *Unification Thought* with Marx, I began to find the answers to my questions. From the moment my questions were answered, I was overwhelmed with the fact that I was a sinner. Dr. Lee saved me. I had a chance to see God. It was so painful that I wanted to commit suicide. *Unification Thought* explained the existence of God to me clearly and in detail. Then a strange fear and terror came upon me and I had no idea what to do.

Then suddenly a giant appeared. I couldn't look at him because of an inexplicable fear. He said to me in a silent voice, "Look at me," and then he walked away without showing his face. I followed him, but he suddenly disappeared. It was very strange. I looked for him further and I found him standing in front of a big picture. He said calmly, "Follow me. It is clear that you must go, find your way, and come up with a solution." But I couldn't stand the fear. I asked Dr. Lee who he was. Dr. Lee told me that he was

Reverend Moon who brought to light the *Divine Principle*. He said that Reverend Moon is the Parent of humankind and explained all the circumstances surrounding that. I couldn't stand the pain. What was I to do? I anguished greatly. But Dr. Lee gave me courage. "As God is the parent and the substance of love, He will forgive everything. Now what you have to do is to follow your mind. God and True Parents lead their children with forgiveness and love." This calmed my mind and gave me courage.

You people on the Earth! Philosophers who think God doesn't exist must brace themselves and observe everything. I experienced the existence of God as the Parent of humankind. And the world after death exists in your future. Please grasp God during your lifetime. If you don't want to anguish in a position as miserable as mine, study the *Divine Principle* and *Unification Thought* and receive Reverend Moon's guidance. I beg that of you. I experienced the message, "Follow me," from Reverend Moon. You people on the Earth! Please attend God and receive Reverend Moon's guidance. I feel that to convey this message is my mission. Please follow my message. Seek for God. He is the Parent of humankind.

Engels, 4.18.2002

Communist Politicians

3. **Lenin** (1870-1924, founder of the Bolsheviks, leader of the Russian Revolution (1917) and the first head of the U.S.S.R.)

"Re-arrange everything as soon as possible."

It is proper if you define me as blind because I insisted that only things we can see exist. My only hope is that all Communists on Earth come to know Godism as soon as possible. After a long interval, I recognized that I was dead and existing in the world of life after death. That was because I couldn't distinguish between life on the Earth and in the spirit world. What kind of place is this? Life here in some ways cannot be distinguished from life on the Earth. For me, who believed that there would be nothing after death, the situation here was very confusing.

But I knew nothing about the eternal spirit. The more I experienced the spirit world, the more I was filled with regret. I live here with the mind of a beggar, drawn into a miasma of countless conflicts. It is natural that Communist countries die out. I had already concluded that somebody would bring down Communist countries on the Earth. I came to know a tremendous truth here.

Dr. Lee, who was taught by Reverend Moon on the Earth, taught me *Unification Thought* and the *Divine Principle* perspective on the cosmos, the world and the shape of future. Because I had lived in a state of confusion for such a long time, I felt pain even as I learned that. No one can accept my stance as a rebel against God. My selfishness and ignorance on the Earth made me like this. But recognizing the truth is ultimately better than forever enduring the pain brought on by ignorance.

God certainly exists. He exists as the Parent of humankind. In spite of that, I put myself on the vanguard of Communist revolution with a sword in my hands, shouting out that there are no parents. I made their hearts ache. I hope all the Communists on the Earth clearly and seriously remember my experience.

Dr. Lee told me that he had no way but to abandon the position of a physician when he learned the *Divine Principle* brought to light by Reverend Moon and was released from all the problems of his life. Dr. Lee lectured on the *Divine Principle* only for me many times and he counseled me directly. One day I felt intolerable suffering in my heart from what I had learned in the *Divine Principle*. To rid myself of the pain, I was walking around. Then I saw an old woman suddenly fall down in front of me. She was bleeding, with her hands grasping a knife stuck in her breast. It occurred to me that I wanted to do something good, so I extended my hands to her and tried to pull out the knife. Suddenly I heard a fearful voice. "I, God, am still alive. You are my child." Only the voice was left and the old woman disappeared. My ears were stunned.

I announce to Communists: God, Jehovah, certainly exists and He is the Parent of humankind. The Communist counties will perish without fail. The ideal of Communism will be realized by its being engrafted upon *Unification Thought*. The important thing is to not be an unfilial child. We are blessed by attending our physical parents, so what can we expect of the people who don't know the way to attend God, the Cosmic Parents? Their fate can be nothing other than a sorrowful death. If you can't believe my words, look at the harmony of nature. Though God is the Creator of nature, how much sincerity do we human beings offer Him? We must know for a surety that humankind has been created as the children of God. I made up my mind to keep my position as a child of God, even though I have such a big deficiency. I have an earnest request for you. There is only one way for Communist countries to live and that is to follow Reverend Moon's guidance. Please study the *Divine Principle* in detail. Please receive the thought of Reverend Moon and study it deeply. If you do so, you will attend God more truly than the thinkers or politicians of the Free World. This is the only way to live truly. If you follow my words, it will release me from unimaginable suffering and agony. I beg this of you. Communist countries must rearrange everything as soon as possible. I met God. The spirit doesn't die, but lives. This is my last wish, given in blood from the world of Heaven. "God is alive. God is the Parent of humankind."

Lenin, 4.19.2002

4. **Stalin** (1879-1953, Lenin's successor as head of the Soviet Union, who communized Russia by force.)

"You must know, believe and attend God."

We live only once on the Earth and in one unique historical period. I was a dictator and a madman. It would have been better had my life on Earth not existed. This is my story in a nutshell. Even after studying *Unification Thought* and the *Divine Principle*, I have not found a way to indemnify my sin. The *Divine Principle* brings me into terrible agony. I have no intention of denying the *Divine Principle*, but because there is no way to save me, I am very sad and in pain.

But I am glad to be given this chance to inform the people on the Earth about the reality of the spirit world. I'd like to tell this to all the Communists on the Earth and appeal to them. Friends in Communist countries, I am Stalin. You have had wrong thinking. As the way you are going is not the way you should go, you must turn to the right path as soon as possible. We Communists lived courageously according to our beliefs, but why could we not control the time of our death? A human being consists of two parts, the physical life and the spiritual life. There is no exception to the rule that all physical bodies die and all spirits go to the eternal world.

One's life on the Earth determines the place one will live in the Heavenly world. Our beliefs are wrong. The worst of it is that we deny and ignore God, who is the origin of the cosmos. Though we are incomplete existences, who know neither the origin nor the destiny of our lives, we shout out loudly that God, the origin of all things, doesn't exist. I suffer with pain here because my life was like that on the Earth. I can't stand this pain.

The God we denied is the Parent of humankind. God is not a theological existence, but is our Parent. How foolish we have been! I am Stalin. You have seen people attending God and celebrating Christmas in your countries. You must have laughed at them, thinking they are weak.

But those at whom we laughed live well in this world. It is certain that they didn't go to Hell. When we laughed at them, they and God loved us. We live in the bottom of Hell here. Do you understand what it means? People here don't treat each other as human beings, but as material. If there were any means to rid myself of this pain, I would do it. The place one dwells in the spirit world cannot be decided by power, honor or gold. It is decided by the sincerity of your life on the Earth. First, know and believe God and attend Him. Second, completely clarify your way of life.

Dr. Lee told me that God forgives everything, as He is the Parent of humankind, but I am still in pain, so I know that I haven't been released yet. Please receive the will of Reverend Moon completely, open your minds and build churches for the worship of God and hold worship services. Reverend Moon reflects the image of God, even though he is a man, and he is struggling intensely to save Communist countries. His thought is messianic, especially for the Communist countries. You must receive his ideology of peace immediately. Because God is alive, only attending God will save the Communist countries.

Friends, please save me. Please liberate me. When your way of life changes according to the teaching of Godism, I will be liberated in the spirit world. God certainly exists. And life in the spirit world is eternal. My heart longs for release from Hell. I, the dictator who denied God, cry out to all the Communist countries on the Earth. Please believe in God and seek for Him. I beg of you for that from the spirit world.

Stalin, 4.19.2002

5. **Leon Trotsky** (1879-1940, a successor of Lenin, defeated by Stalin in the struggle for succession. An assassin sent by Stalin killed him while in exile in Mexico.)

"I want to burn up atheistic materialism completely."

I know that the *Divine Principle* is God's truth that is brought to light by Reverend Moon through revelation. But even before I learned *Unification Thought* and the *Divine Principle*, I realized I had lived wrongly. From the moment I realized that I was in the spirit world, I repented of my life on the Earth. If there is nothing after death, man is no different from animals.

My life on the Earth was not that of a man, but of a cow or pig. Please realize that I compared myself with animals. How comfortable animals must be without self-consciousness! I didn't know God. I didn't deny God, but I didn't think about nor feel agony about God or spiritual matters. But my spirit certainly is alive here, so I can't help thinking on it.

How can I clarify my sin? I lived as a leader of Communists standing for atheism. To find the way is very difficult. Thinking about my spiritual life, I'd like to burn up atheistic materialism completely, not even by *Unification Thought* or the *Divine Principle*. I have been regretting my life on the Earth in misery and extreme sorrow. I even envy animals, which don't entertain thoughts.

Please forgive me, God. I lived a wrongful life on the Earth. God is the Parent of humankind. Can you forgive my extremely unfilial behavior? Reverend Moon, True Parents of humankind and Father of humankind! Please save the Communist countries! And please teach Godism to them thoroughly. I will lay the indemnity conditions for my sinful life. I thoroughly believe God clearly exists and is the Parent of humankind.

Trotsky, 4.19.2002

6. **Nikita Khrushchev** (1894-1971, a chief secretary of the
Russian Communist Party; criticized Stalin.)

"The Communist countries will perish without fail."

People in the Communist countries lived their lives thinking
that there is nothing after death. I lived my life like that, too. But
when I look at myself in the spirit world, I feel weary. There is no
meaning to regretting my life on the Earth, but I feel thoroughly
that it was not a truly human life. I feel that I should disappear to
a place where nobody can go for a long time.

God actually exists. I can't understand why human beings do
not treat each other as human, or why they don't reflect upon their
human shape in the mirror, in spite of the fact that they are God's
creation. Even God longs for human beings to realize His ideal existence as the Creator. I realized that Communism is a very fearful
thought after I got here. Many intellectuals influenced by
Communism must change their atheistic way of thinking as soon
as possible when they arrive here, as they see that their lives are
reported on here.

If you can't believe it, think about the way human beings are
built. Human beings have dual characteristics. They have mind
and body. The order of the mind is different from that of body. It
is a fact that there is a spirit world where the mind can live. God is
the master of the mind, and He has been the Parent of humankind
from the beginning, and we have been His children. If you ignore
this, thinking it unreasonable, you will inevitably become a sad
miserable and suffering spirit like us. It's up to you. But
Communist countries will perish without fail. They won't just
perish, but miserably perish. That is because God exists and He is
the Parent of humankind. It is very natural for Communism, which
denies God's existence and treats humankind as material, to perish.

Communists on the Earth: please look at the lives of
Christians. God is there and feels pain in His heart looking at His
children who follow the Communist paradigm and live without
knowing their parents. You must prepare to live attending God as
soon as possible. The Communist countries on the Earth will
perish. I found this fact thoroughly confirmed here in the spirit
world. Reverend Moon on the Earth is the one whom God sent to

save Communists, and he is the Messiah and True Parents.

The Communist countries will revive by learning his thought and being guided by him. Please change your way of life to that of Godism. Abandon the Communist way of thinking. If you go on, not only your lives on the Earth will end, but also your spiritual life will thoroughly collapse. There is no way to live under Communism. God exists and the spirit world certainly exists. I'd truly like to appeal from the spirit world for the Communist countries to change direction.

Khrushchev, 4.19.2002

7. **Leonid Brezhnev** (1906-1982, a chief secretary of the Russian Communist Party; a Communist of the Stalinist type.)

"When Communist countries receive Godism, they will revive."

I'm grateful that I, who couldn't treat humankind according to our real value, was forgiven so that I can be included among the people. I'm also grateful that I was given a chance like this. Members and followers of the Communist Party, politicians, thinkers in Communist countries! I'd like to tell you from the spirit world of the wrongness of my life on the Earth. Please receive this seriously and clarify the priorities in your lives as soon as possible.

I didn't know of God's existence, nor did I recognize Him. I treated His children as if they were animals. I can't escape from my sin and the punishment that it brings. As I treated precious human beings as animals, I live here in a zoo. Do you understand what it means? Only animals live in a zoo. I live with them. Though my form is that of a human being with five senses, I live like an animal, eating with animals. Can you imagine how I feel?

Friends, God exists. All human beings are His precious children. And the physical body is necessary only on the Earth. Death is not the end of life, but there is the spirit world where the spirits of humankind live. Nobody interferes here in the spirit world. Also one's position here is decided by the quality of one's life on the Earth.

Comrades! I want to live with people. Trying to live with animals, I crawled on my hands and feet as an animal does. I was so lonely that I wanted to be friends with animals. So I tried to eat as an animal does instead of with my hands. I can describe my life here. When I was on the Earth, I insisted that God doesn't exist and I couldn't exhibit an authentic human nature. But if I correct your life on Earth by informing you of the facts here, then I can live with human beings here.

Comrades! Communists place themselves under God's curse. Please leave it behind as soon as possible. You will perish if you don't. I checked out the facts thoroughly. I can be released after you change and center your lives on God. Comrades! Don't be miserable like me. Please escape from your old lives now. You must live where people live even if it gives you a lot of difficulties. That is what I wish most.

Comrades! This is the last favor I request. You must know clearly that God is the Parent of humankind. Reverend Moon has appeared on the Earth in order to save Communist countries with the mission of True Parents. God sent him and he is the Messiah for those suffering under Communism. You can live by following him and receiving guidance from him. Communist countries must apply *Unification Thought* and the *Divine Principle* in their organization. This is the only way your governments can be revived. If not, they will perish; not just perish, but die a miserable death. This is my serious cry from the spirit world. Please change your way of thinking to that of Godism as soon as possible.

Brezhnev, 4.20.2002

8. **Mao Tse Tung** (1893-1976, built the socialist society in China.)

"I will thoroughly apply Godism in my life."
If I could only return to the Earth, I would live as a true man. If there were somewhere invisible, I would hide myself there. I wished to have my followers worship me rather than God. I longed for them to worship me rather than God, even if He exists. How could a man such as me stand as a god with my mouth?

The four great saints tried to comfort me, telling me that God, as the Parent of humankind, forgives everything. Introducing *Unification Thought* and the *Divine Principle*, they kindly explained the mental suffering they endured until they unified in every respect. It was a very short period, but I was treated as a man. I would like to tell clearly to all the Christians and Communists on the Earth how I live here. I lived under an old tree, because everybody hated me. It was the only place I could hide. I lived under the old tree avoiding the hot and cold weather. I bet you can imagine the shape I was in. I feel liberated now that I have honestly talked to you.

My friends and all people! Human beings will perish if they do not follow Godism. God exists and the spirit world clearly exists. Reverend Moon, True Parents, who illuminated the truth that God is the Parent of humankind, please save our Communist people. Thank you for the hard work and love you invest to save humankind by God's special order. As I am saved, I will live thoroughly according to Godism. Thank you.

Mao Tse Tung, 4.20.2002*

* Message from Dr. Lee: The four great saints and the leaders of the five major religions, who learned *Divine Principle*, visit the Communist leaders directly and ask them actively to participate in the seminar. Mohammad displays enthusiasm, lectures the *Divine Principle*, and helps me a lot. The reporter, Young Soon Kim.

9. **Zhou Enlai** (1898-1976, first premier of the People's Republic of China.)

"Communism is not the truth."

I was thinking I was punished for not believing in but even at the same time not ignoring God. Under God's curse, I was unable to speak, but now I am blessed to be able to speak, and I'm grateful for that.

I shouted out loudly that God doesn't exist, but there was always fear and anxiety in my mind. I thought, "Is it true that God doesn't exist?" This was the voice of my mind that didn't want to betray God. Power and the honor were needed only for short time on the Earth. But I lived ignoring the impact it would have for me in the spirit world.

The pain that I felt as a mute here was serious. Many times people misunderstood me and hit me because I couldn't express myself. I was always lonely, too. How good it would have been were the power and honor I enjoyed on the Earth effective here, too!

Friends of the Communist Party! Heaven punished me for betraying God. God did not give the curse and the punishment. One goes the way one must by oneself. I don't think I can make you understand the true situation here. I'd like to give my last wish to you members of the Communist Party. Remember nothing but this. God exists. He exists as the Parent of humankind. I'd like to ask of you a favor from the spirit world. The spirit world certainly exists. What you must especially remember is to be guided by Reverend Moon on the Earth.

Members of the Communist Party! You can live only if you abandon atheistic materialism with all haste. That belief system makes not only the body die, but also the spirit. If you don't abandon it, you will suffer in a miserable realm of spirit world. As Reverend Moon is the Messiah, the True Parents and the teacher of humankind sent to save Communist countries in this age, please follow Him immediately. He is very old now. I ask you to do this from Heaven. The one who commits sin will be punished. God is the Parent of humankind, and humankind is His children and brothers and sisters to each other. Communism will perish, because it is not the truth.

Zhou Enlai, 4.21.2002

10. **Deng Xiaoping** (1902-1997, the Chairman of the Chinese Communist Party.)

"Communism leads humankind in the wrong direction."

Thanks be to God for forgiving the one who committed sin. Thank you, Reverend Moon, for working hard to save those in Hell and the Communist bloc. I participated here earnestly longing for the members of the Communist Party to make a new start.

When I came here from the Earth, scores of angels guided me. I felt as if they were leading me. Being led by them, I really felt that my power was of no use. They disappeared, depositing me in this place without a single word.

There was nobody here and nothing but a swampy ditch. I wondered where I was. I looked around, but I couldn't find anyone. There was nothing but the swamp. I couldn't leave. It was a fearful place and the swamp seemed to be ready to swallow me if I moved the slightest bit. I was hungry and it was cold at times and hot at other times. Sometimes the darkness turned into a storm. There was the sound of unlimited loneliness and anxiety in my mind. If a man commits a sin, he will be punished.

Where was it? It was the place the spirits live. I wandered in this pain, loneliness and anxiety for many days. Then one day there appeared my Messiah. He was the one Jesus sent to retrieve me. Following his invitation, I came to listen to a very precious lecture. It was on *Unification Thought* and the *Divine Principle*. I was beside myself. The lectures told me that Reverend Moon is the Messiah of humankind and that God is the Parent of humankind, and that he is working so hard to save Communist countries. It shocked me and made my heart sorely ache.

I lived a very harsh life here, staying away from God in a place that has nothing to do with Him, not attending Him. I understand now the effects of love, respect, faith and sincerity. And I think I know why all the religions have become one as brothers and sisters.

Friends in the Communist Party! The word that followed me was one that made God's heart bleed. I now know that I was a terrible sinner. Reverend Moon is the one who brought to light *Unification Thought* and the *Divine Principle*. Follow him and be guided by him. Communism has misled humankind. God exists as the Parent of humankind. We all became rebels against God. The spirits are destined to live here in the spirit world. There is no way for Communists to live except by following Reverend Moon's guidance. This is my earnest wish and appeal. Now that I have been released from the dank swamp, I will attend God and live earnestly.

Deng Xiaoping, 4.21.2002

11. **Erich Honecker** (1912-1994, chairman of the East German Communist Party, ordered the building of the Berlin Wall.)

"Well manage a new life centering on Godism."
After pounding a nail into God's heart, I stood here in spite of building the Berlin Wall. Friends of Communism! Communist countries will perish. You must renew your way of thinking by

seeing the lives of the Russian and Chinese Communist leaders here. How could these things be worked out except by God's great power?

Comrades! Power, honor and material things have less value than garbage here. They are totally useless. You must remember this. God exists. God is the Parent of humankind. And the spirit world exists. If you live rightly, you will live in a good place here, but if you do not, you will be punished. Do the Communist leaders live in good places? Or do they live in Hell as their punishment? That is up to you. But please remember to receive the guidance of Reverend Moon on the Earth. He is the Messiah for Communist countries. You will live if you follow him, but absolutely perish if you don't. He brought the four great saints and major religions into oneness centering on the *Divine Principle*. I will manage a new life here centering on Godism.

Honecker, 4.21.2002

12. **Nicolae Ceaucescu** (1918-1989, a dictator controlling the Rumanian Communist government.)

"I clearly experienced the way of Heaven."

If you throw your eyes, mouth, nose and other sense organs into a compost heap, the smell that comes as they go bad is worse than that of fish. Why did I live like this? It is useless to repent for it now, but I'd like to make people realize that Communism is wrong by showing the reality of the shape I'm in here. As my punishment, I live in a place of thieves. There is no place where I can sit. There is nothing that is mine. I sit down and get up and soon see a man sitting where I was sitting. I lie down and get up, then a man sits there and shouts that it is his place. He calls me a thief and tells me to go away. How can I express this? I long for a place where I can peacefully sit. I always have to keep standing up. The blood vessels in my legs are about to burst. You will be punished if you live as I did; that is why I reveal my situation clearly. I want to tell you that there is a world after death and that God certainly exists. We can't see Him, but He does exist. So if you commit sin, you will be punished. God doesn't give the punishment. I came here of my own will, as a season on the Earth arrives of its own nature. It is like the magnetic needle on a compass. Otherwise why wouldn't I think of going to a better place?

Dictatorial power is useless here. Power and having a state apparatus have less value than trash. There is no use for them. And God exists. He is the Parent of humankind. I punished myself. I was punishing myself thoroughly. Communism certainly will perish. Dictatorship will perish. They must disappear as soon as possible. It is being proven as a fact on Earth.

Members of the Communist parties! Leaders of the Communist parties! Please uproot the wrong ideas of Communism as soon as possible. And this is my last favor. The only way for Communists to survive is to follow Reverend Moon's guidance. He is the Messiah sent by God to save the Communist countries. You can live only if you grasp him. I will absolutely follow God. I realized clearly that it is the way of Heaven. I will begin anew with Godism.

Ceaucescu, 4.22.2002

13. **Ho Chi-Minh** (1890-1969, leader of the Vietnamese Communist Party. He repelled United States forces during the Vietnam War and brought about the unification of North and South Vietnam under Communism.)

"The Unification Principle is the hope and torchlight for all humanity."

I, Ho Chi-Minh, lived in a very wrong way when I was on Earth. I struggled for decades to bring about national liberation, but because I was unable to find an ideology that was correct, I ended up creating one of the poorest countries on Earth. I do not want to spend even a moment in this place thinking about my life on Earth. I am truly grateful that I was called to attend this seminar in spite of everything. Through the Unification Principle education I received, I have come to understand a new view of life and world-view. Now I want to cut myself off from all my past without hesitation, and live in attendance to God as my Parent. The Unification Principle is the hope and torchlight for all humanity. The Unification Principle clearly reveals the errors of Communism.

Reverend Sun Myung Moon, True Parents! Please save us

brothers who are wandering about from place to place because we have no suitable dwelling place. In this seminar, I have come to know God and to deeply understand humanity's life after death. Please guide the Communist leaders on Earth so that they, too, may lead correct lives centering on Godism.

Ho Chi-Minh, 4.24.2002

14. **Pol Pot** (1925-1998, leader of the Cambodian Khmer Rouge. He carried out the slaughter of some 2 million people.)

"You, too, must change to a worldview and view of human life that is centered on Godism."

During my life on Earth, I, Pol Pot, treated human life as if it were merely material existence, in accordance with the Communist view of life. Therefore, I indiscriminately executed those who opposed the ideology of Party members. For this reason, in my existence here I cannot be treated as a human being. I cannot escape the consequence of the sin of having slaughtered such a large number of God's children... Communist leaders on Earth! It gives me much shame to say this, but in this place I am living with a pony. I have been allotted very little time, so I cannot explain much about my situation here, only that I am constrained such that whenever the pony jumps, I must jump with it.

I tell you that through the Unification Principle I have come to a definite realization about life after death and the existence of God. It is the final chance for us Communists to survive. It provides Communist Party members with one last chance to repent for having denied God. All Communist Party members here can receive the opportunity for new life by attending the Unification Principle seminar. I acknowledge the existence of God, and clearly reveal to you my situation in the afterlife. My message to you on Earth is that you, too, must change to a worldview and view of human life that is centered on Godism. Only when you do this will the Communist Party members who are now in Hell in the spirit world be liberated. I have one final sincere appeal. It is that Communist Party members understand that Reverend Moon's way is the only way for you to follow from now on. He is the True

Parent of humankind, and you must follow his teachings. This is the only way that Communist countries can survive. People on Earth, please bear this in mind.

Pol Pot, 4.24.2002

15. **Che Guevara** (1928-1967, a leader of the Communist revolution in Cuba; he later separated from Castro. He took part in the struggle for a Communist revolution in Bolivia and was shot dead by Bolivian government forces.)

"I thoroughly repent for my life as a revolutionary on Earth, because it was based on a wrong ideology."

I, Che Guevara, acknowledge the existence of God, and experience that there is a world of the soul. I cannot help but point out that Marxist philosophy contains many errors. I declare to all Heaven and Earth that God and human beings are in a relationship of parent and child. I thoroughly repent for my life on Earth as a revolutionary, because it was based on a wrong ideology. I firmly pledge that I will become a child of God.

I am convinced that Reverend Moon is the True Parent of humankind.

Che Guevara, 4.25.2002

Messages from 12 Journalists
representing 120 World Journalists

1. **Hugh Love** Died 2002 at age 73. Belfast Telegraph reporter, UK

"Jesus asked me to report on the situation here to people on earth. "

I, Hugh Love, would like to file a news flash to the earth from the spirit world, the world after death. I believe the fact that I am able to do this is already shocking news. Here, I've experienced something unimaginable. I met Jesus, who is adored not only by all Christians but also by all humanity He greeted me, "Welcome. You're new here, aren't you?" and treated me with utmost kindness.

He then continued, "As people on earth are not acquainted with the actual situation here in the spirit world, I would like you to report it factually to them so that when they come here, their souls may have definite knowledge of the place where they can remain with God." In order to fulfill this request, I would like to submit as accurate a report as possible of the events taking place here to the people on earth.

I could not understand what was happening that so many people would be gathered here. As soon as I entered the place, cameras began to flash all around. Although I had been a reporter on earth, I was not a cameraman and therefore had never taken pictures. In one place, a person I did not recognize kept taking pictures with a flash, and the flashes of light made me feel dizzy. How should I report these things to people on earth? There were many people in this place, but it was very quiet. I did not dare to breathe too loudly. This place is a lecture facility were the Divine Principle is conveyed. It is a place where lectures are given on the Divine Principle and Unification Thought, which God had revealed to Reverend Sun Myung Moon, the founder of the Unification Church who is on earth. The atmosphere surrounding the lecturers and the audience was more sober than anything I had ever seen before. I was so affected by the atmosphere that it was difficult for me to cover the event. I did not feel I could walk around as I pleased.

The lecturers explained to me that the camera flashes had been my momentary spiritual experience, and the flashing light that I saw was a manifestation of God. I also listened to the Divine Principle lecture, but for the most part I paid little attention to the contents. The topics and contents of the Divine Principle lecture were unfamiliar to me. Perhaps because it has not been long since I left the earth, I find it amazing that such things as these are going on in the spirit world. It is incredibly mysterious. Oh! How can this be? Most people in the audience looked enraptured by the Divine Principle lecture. It appeared clear that some superhuman power was at work.

Outside the lecture room, a sea of people waited their turn to enter, and the atmosphere inside the room was solemn and sober. I am not yet ready to gather information on the profound depth of the Divine Principle. As a reporter, I can only convey the atmosphere of this place to people on earth.

I saw Jesus sitting humbly in a respectful posture in the front row. It appeared to me that there was something in this place that humankind has never experienced before ? some kind of secret of Heaven. I cannot rid myself of the desire to step out of my position as a journalist and study the Divine Principle.

Hugh Love, 14 May 2002

2. **Fernando Pessa** 1902-2002.

The well-known RTP and BBC Radio commentator was hailed as the world's oldest journalist when he died the previous month in Portugal, a fortnight after celebrating his hundredth birthday. This well-liked reporter made a name for himself when broadcasting during World War II for the BBC, for which he was subsequently decorated by King George VI with the Order of the British Empire (OBE). He then went on to launch Portugal's radio and TV system (RTP).

"It is my infinite honor to gather information about this place and report it to you."

Special news bulletin to people on earth! This is the heavenly world. Because there is news here so incredible as to be beyond the imagination of people on earth, I, Fernando Pessa, act on my professional spirit and convey this news to people on earth. Generally speaking, during their lifetime, people are unable to either definitely affirm or reject the existence of a world after death. Most people just live with the question, "I wonder if it exists?"

People on earth, I will definitely prove to you that the world after death exists. Recently, a special bridge was established so that messages can be conveyed to the earthly world. This is generally not possible, but it has been made possible now by the special consideration of the Reverend Sun Myung Moon, who is on the earth. It is possible only for a special period for the purpose of telling people on earth about the existence of God and the world after death. Reverend Sun Myung Moon has been manifested on the earth as the True Parent of the heavenly and earthly worlds for the purpose of bringing about a world of peace centered on God. I am now in a place where religious leaders of various levels and communist leaders are receiving education in the Divine Principle by special invitation. There is a sea of people gathered here. Among the several unique features of this place is that order is very well maintained, despite the presence of thousands of people. It is so well maintained that it seems strange. Nothing on earth compares with this. Another unique feature is that everyone without exception, after receiving the Divine Principle education, comes to a realization about the original state of human beings and the fundamental direction of life and becomes a new person. A third is that there is a total absence of any barriers between religions and races.

Neither are there any conflicts among ideologies. The representatives of the four major religions - Jesus, Confucius, Buddha and Mohammed, as well as St. Augustine, Socrates, and recently communist leaders including Marx, Engels, Lenin and Stalin are gathered here together. Here one can meet all the famous people who have appeared in the course of human history. People on earth, isn't this incredible? They sometimes guide newcomers and give them encouragement. Some of them speak directly about the life of the Reverend Sun Myung Moon, who revealed the Divine Principle and Unification Thought.

This is a unique place where all these people have torn down all barriers between religions, races and philosophies. They love and respect each other; they are all one with each other. What deep content does the Divine Principle hold that such things are possible? People on earth, I consider it an infinite honor that I am able to gather news about this unique situation and report it to you. It is of greater honor than anything I ever experienced during my earthly life. I have not the slightest doubt that if everyone could become one by the power of the truth and of love, as is happening here, peace would certainly come to all humanity on earth as well.

I hope that those people on earth who are lacking in their belief in the world after death and the existence of God will not ignore what is happening here. If people in the earthly world would do as is happening here in the heavenly world ? that is, break down the walls between religions, races, and ideologies, and live centering upon God ? then all the confrontations, friction, conflicts, and wars would naturally disappear. Let us put our heads together and find out about the power of the Divine Principle.

Fernando Pessa, 14 May 2002

3. Esau Jaramillo A well-known sports reporter in Columbia.

"I much deplore not being able to interview the Four Great Saints about their impressions." When Esau Jaramillo was alive on earth, he never handled a scoop like this.

Really, this is the most amazing and shocking scoop in all human history. When will there be another opportunity to send a story from the heavenly world to the earthly world? People on earth, please listen carefully to this news. This is the heavenly world, where the so-called spirit lives eternally after human beings die. Here, I've met the Four Great Saints, Jesus, Buddha, Confucius, and Mohammed. The leaders of various religious groups come and go freely and live here. In particular, there is a Divine Principle lecture facility here. The Divine Principle is God's revelation, and the new truth for the twenty-first century revealed by the Reverend Sun Myung Moon.

According to the Divine Principle, Reverend Sun Myung Moon is the Messiah and Savior of humankind and the True Parent of Heaven and Earth. The founders of the four major religions attend Reverend Sun Myung Moon as their True Parent, and believe absolutely in the Divine Principle. This place qualifies to be called Heaven.

People here live as brothers and sisters. They always live harmoniously as members of one family, respecting and loving each other, and doing things for each other. They are kind and warm even to those who come here for the first time. Thousands gather to listen to the lectures on the Divine Principle, but they do not talk among themselves and the atmosphere is quite solemn and serious. Anyone who experiences this atmosphere would find it overpowering. I deplore very much not being able to interview the Four Great Saints about their impressions. I intend to study how it is that people are born again as new people after they are educated in the Divine Principle.

When that becomes clear, I will send another exclusive story to people on earth.

Esau Jaramillo, 15 May 2002

4. **Clem Lloyd** Died on last New Year's Eve at age 62. One of Australia's leading journalists and journalism educators. Worked for almost fifteen years as chief of staff and press secretary for leaders of the Australian Federal Labor Party. Research professor at Canberra University. Appointed an Officer in the Order of Australia (AO) in 1993 for services to public policy public administration, journalism and education.

"Can it be that the peace of humankind begins with the Divine Principle?"

The lecture facility with the strange sign saying "Divine Principle Study Facility" always has many people coming and going. It is a place where mysterious miracles take place every day. I cannot give too much praise to the courtesy, geniality and order-liness shown by the participants here.

There is a new revolution in human character transpiring here. I, Clem Lloyd had heard the common rumors when I began to gather information. The moment I set foot in the lecture hall, I could not help but be surprised again by the solemn and quiet atmosphere of the lecture hall. Although many people are listening to the Divine Principle lecture, it is so quiet that one can hear a pin drop. The only sound is the voice of the lecturer that resonates in a harmonious union of excitement, heart and passion. It was like an orchestra in concert. In the lecture hall, my heart was struck by the placard carrying the theme "God is the Parent of All Humankind." Here and there, I could see people trying hard to hold back tears. I myself, having been completely immersed in this atmosphere, began to shed tears.

What did it mean that God is the Parent of humankind? And what did it mean that the Reverend Sun Myung Moon is the Messiah, Savior and True Parent of all humankind? I quietly took a seat so as to listen to the lecture. The more deeply I became involved in the lecture, the more I was moved. I continued to shed tears, though I did not understand why. It is very difficult for me to describe this in a few words. Suffice it to say that the content of the lecture was completely new, and it was well organized. This was the Divine Principle. According to the explanation of the lecturers, the person who revealed the Divine Principle is the Messiah and True Parent of all humankind, and his name is Sun Myung Moon. The Divine Principle is something out of the ordinary. I cannot suppress an intellectual curiosity that makes me want to study it further. Can it be that the peace of humankind begins with the Divine Principle? I leave that up to the judgement of readers on earth.

Clem Lloyd, 15 May 2002

5. **Donald Woods** Died 2001 at age 67. Veteran South African newspaper editor and anti-apartheid activist. Africa). Returned to South Africa in August 1990 after 13 years in exile. Made a Commander of the British Empire (CBE) by Queen Elizabeth II in 2000 for his human rights activities.

"All roads lead to the Divine Principle."
Freedom of the press is protected in the earthly world for appearances' sake but it is not protected a hundred percent. Right now in the heavenly world, I, Donald Woods am able to gather news on anything without anyone's control or interference. Freedom of the press is completely protected in the heavenly world. I intend to report to the earthly world exactly what I see and feel

concerning the situation here. Very shocking things are happening here.

People on earth! This is the heavenly world. I have received the special grace to convey a message from the place where the souls reside, that is, the world after death, to the earthly world. What is the Divine Principle? In short, it is the doctrine of the Unification Church, revealed by the Reverend Sun Myung Moon through a revelation from God. Actually, though, it would be much better to refer to it as a truth that transcends all religions philosophies and races. This is because religious leaders, philosophers and politicians of many dimensions have all changed to become new people after hearing the Divine Principle.

For example, the representatives of the four major religions have formed a oneness with each other centering on the Divine Principle, and are cooperating with each other on all their activities. In the earthly world, there was once a saying, "All roads lead to Rome." Here in the heavenly world, I believe a new proposition will soon appear that says, "All roads lead to the Divine Principle." I would like to find out the details of what has made it this way. In this place, I met personally with Mohammed, the Prophet of Islam. This was a totally unexpected development. What was particularly amazing was that he is now the director in charge of the Divine Principle Education Program. When did he come to be this way? That is a complete mystery. People in the world adored him, so why is he working here in this way? I am most concerned about the reaction of Muslims on earth when they learn this fact. How can the realities of the earthly world and heavenly world be so different? It is only to be expected that earthly people will not believe these things. In fact, I, too, have experienced these things directly, finding them hard to believe. I only report these facts. Mohammed is the very essence of gentleness, humility and kindness. In this place alone, there appear to be no walls between religions, races or philosophies. In this place, all have become one. Here, one can truly experience joy, happiness, peace, freedom, equality and righteousness for the first time. There are so many interesting stories for me here that I cannot bear to leave.

Donald Woods, 15 May 2002

6. **Sailen Chatterjee** Died 2001at age 78. Journalist, freedom fighter and a close associate of Mahatma Gandhi. Long remembered for his coverage of Gandhiji's peace mission in Noakhali district of undivided Bengal from December 1946 to March 1947, which greatly restored the confidence of the people. Chatterjee, then only 23, toured the villages barefoot with Gandhiji braving communal violence.

"The new typhoon of the Unification Movement is blowing here in this place."

In this heavenly world, I, Sailen Chatterjee, have been able to do something that I wanted to do all my life. I came to the Divine Principle lecture facility. This place transcends the many barriers that one often experiences on earth. It is a place where the Divine Principle is taught so that people can live freely and in peace. The Divine Principle can be seen as the teachings of one particular religion, but anyone who examines its contents in detail finds that it is a fundamental teaching about God, the universe, and human life. Of course, I, too, received Divine Principle education here.

Representatives of the various religions, general leaders and intellectuals are gathered here. They are always discussing and sharing their opinions with each other freely and peacefully.

The most amazing fact here is that famous saints and sages from human history come and go as they please and are cooperating with the educational proceedings with enthusiasm. The Divine Principle appears to contain the necessary elements for manifesting humanity's peaceful world for all.

According to the Four Great Saints here, the Divine Principle is the truth revealed by the Reverend Sun Myung Moon of the Unification Church through a revelation from God, and anyone who receives Divine Principle education will be reborn as a new person. The new typhoon of the Unification Movement is blowing in this place. No one can predict what results the Unification Movement will bring to this place.

I, too, will actively participate in this movement. Also, it appears it would not be unreasonable for people on earth to believe that the Reverend Sun Myung Moon is the Messiah and Savior of all humankind. From what I have seen here, this can be easily substantiated. All the people here, without exception, are free and peaceful. The Four Great Saints are walking the path of being examples of the Divine Principle. I am truly glad that I am given the chance to do things here that I was not able to complete on earth.

Sailen Chatterjee, 16 May 2002

7. **Igor Alexandrov** Investigative journalist. Brutally murdered in Slavyansk, Ukraine on 3 July 2001 by unknown assailants in one of a series of violent incidents involving journalists.

"The Divine Principle will bring about a paradigm shift for traditional theology."

We are not able to have definite knowledge of the existence of God. We only live with the supposition, "He must exist." It is possible for us logically to deny God's existence, but it would probably be impossible for us to deny His existence in our actual daily lives. What can this God be? I, Igor Alexandrov, am no longer living on earth. I live in the world after death, which has always been the object of people's curiosity. Not having been here long, I am not yet accustomed to the phenomena here. I was given a special grace, allowing me to report from the heavenly world to the earthly world, I find it quite novel that things which cannot normally be experienced on earth are occurring here in the heavenly world.

Divine Principle education must be going on in many places in the earthly world as well. Having received it here, I would like to report briefly on my own views regarding the existence of God. The Divine Principle, under the overall theme "God is the Parent of Humankind," explains in amazing details God's attributes, the relationship among them, the motivation for His creation of the universe, its method and purpose, and innumerable other matters. This content is truly original and the presentation is very logical. Things are described in terms not of probability but certainty. The Divine Principle explains that God exists as the unified body of the dual characteristics of internal nature and external form and the harmonized union of masculinity and feminity. I cannot begin to explain the shock and excitement that this proposition gives me. I believe it will bring about a paradigm shift for traditional theology in particular.

The Divine Principle is causing human consciousness to evolve to a new dimension.

Thousands have gathered here to listen to the lectures, but they exhibit an exceedingly disciplined attitude toward their education. God is the Parent of humankind, and we are all brothers and sisters. This is the prerequisite for humanity to bring about a world of peace. I now am certain that this will be realized by the Divine Principle, which is the new truth of the new age of the new millennium brought to light by the Reverend Sun Myung Moon who received God's revelation. I regret that I cannot introduce all the sections of the Divine Principle at this time. I look forward to the day when the heavenly world and the earthly world are one.

Igor Alexandrov, 16 May 2002

8. Charles Templeton   1915-2001. Died at age 85. Canada's legendary newspaper and magazine reporter, and CBC and CTV broadcaster and news director.

Received two ACTRA (Association of Canadian Radio and Television Artists) awards and the B'nai Brith award in 1967. As a young man, he quickly rose to the top of Protestant evangelism together with his close friend Billy Graham in the 1940s, but later went to the seminary and came out an agnostic. In 1995, he published a book entitled "Farewell to God: My Reasons for Rejecting the Christian Faith."

"I am inspired by the greatness of the Divine Principle in its ability to unite the Four Great Saints as one."

There seems to be no accepted theory as to the world of the human soul. I, Charles Templeton, am now sending a message from the heavenly world, that is the world after death. It would give me utmost pleasure if this message were to aid people on earth in improving their understanding of the world after death.

I am now in the Divine Principle lecture facility in the heavenly world. I will report to you on the unique life and incidents here. In the earthly world, there are many religions and denominations, and sometimes there is confrontation and friction among these. Here, though, there is no such thing What is particularly surprising is that the Four Great Saints of the four major religions - Christianity (Jesus), Confucianism (Confucius), Buddhism (Buddha) and Islam (Mohammed) - are together here. I don't know if I will ever have another opportunity here to meet such great saints. Despite my humble position, I ventured to ask them, "What is it that made you one?" Jesus answered me, saying, "The Reverend Sun Myung Moon is the Savior, Messiah and True Parent of humankind. So it is only natural for us to accept the philosophy and guidance of the Messiah. I, Jesus, was the Messiah of the New Testament Age, but the Messiah of the Completed Testament Age is the Reverend Sun Myung Moon. Yet my mission and his mission from the viewpoint of God's will, are one and the same." I still do not understand the meaning of Jesus' words. I do know that most of what the saints said is the same as what Jesus said.

Confucius said, "God is the vertical True Parent of humankind, and the Reverend Sun Myung Moon is the horizontal True Parent. Also, all people belong to one brotherhood and sisterhood. The Divine Principle has made this clear from many aspects. All people, without exception, must become one with one another centering on the True Parents." I do not understand what Confucius meant when he referred to vertical and horizontal True Parents. Buddha answered me, saying, "Until now, the teachings of Buddhism were very vague on the fundamental reason for God's creation of the universe. Rev. Sun Myung Moon, the Messiah of humankind, has now taught us this through the Divine Principle. He has also taught us clearly about what human beings are and about human life. It should not be strange at all that we have become one with each other through the new truth." Buddha's reply made me feel that I had asked a very obvious question.

Mohammed spoke to me as follows: "The Divine Principle makes it completely clear that Allah (the absolute God of Islam) and God (the absolute God of Christianity) are one substantial Being. So the teachings of Christianity and those of Islam are fundamentally one. The teaching with the greater realistic meaning is that which says that God is the Parent of humankind, and that all human beings are His children. Also, the Reverend Sun Myung Moon is the Savior, Messiah and True Parent of humankind. With the appearance of this new truth, we can but only move toward oneness. We always belonged to one brotherhood and one sisterhood, but we did not know this until now, and this is the reason so many religious bodies and denominations came into being. We have all become one in God's love and truth. Now that we have done so and experienced resulting peace and happiness, we wonder why we were not able to do this before. The earthly world must become one, too, in the same way as the heavenly world. We human beings can become one only when we live in attendance of the True Parents."

In any case, these were their answers. I have yet to grasp the true meaning of their statements. I am merely reporting to you their replies as they gave them. They were all very gentle and humble. More than anything else, it was the Divine Principle that brought them together as one. I would like to emulate their character. I hope this will be of assistance to your lives in the earthly world.

Charles Templeton, 16 May 2002

9. **Alexandre Jose Barbosa Lima Sobrinho** Died 2000 at age 103. Longtime president of the Brazilian Press Association of Brazil and believed to be the world's oldest practicing writer. Opposed the military administration and defied corrupt politicians and wrongdoers. Was a three-time congressman and governor of the northeastern state of Pernambuco Ran for vice-president in 1974.

"Now the True Parents are guiding both the heavenly and earthly worlds."

I, Barbosa Lima, have received not a small amount of excitement and deep emotion as I witnessed the scene here in the heavenly world of an education that is unprecedented in human history. Large crowds of people continuously come and go here. I was curious about the type of activity going on in this place, so I met the person responsible. He immediately understood what I was trying to do, and responded to me with candor and kindness as he explained about the Divine Principle education. He introduced himself as Sang Hun Lee.

According to teacher Lee, this facility provides education in the Divine Principle, which was revealed by the Reverend Sun

Myung Moon through a revelation from God. As he explained to me the topics of the Divine Principle one by one, he gave me a philosophical perspective on the fundamental reason that we human beings have not been able to become one.

The Reverend Sun Myung Moon currently is in the earthly world, but he is the Messiah and True Parents of humankind, who directly controls the various realities of the heavenly world as well. Teacher Lee told me that this place provides Divine Principle education, in accordance with directions from the True Parents, to religious and political leaders, philosophers and leaders in other fields who have exercised a degree of influence in human history. He said that when the educational program was first launched, there were quite a few who did not understand its significance and were reluctant to attend, but now there are so many prospective participants that it is provided only to those who are specifically chosen. I am unable to record here the full content of the Divine Principle lecture that I received from him, but it seemed to reveal surprising facts about God, humanity and nature In any case, there can be no doubt that many people are being renewed through Divine Principle education. I feel that I, too, have been assimilated to a great extent by teacher Lee's sincere and passionate explanations, and his humble demeanor. I keep feeling a strong urge within me to listen to the Divine Principle lectures at the next opportunity.

Alexandre Jose Barbosa Lima Sobrinho, 16 May 2002

10. **Peter Smark** 1936-2000. Died at age 63. Famous Australian journalist who worked for AAP-Reuters, The Australian, The Age, and The Sydney Morning Herald as a foreign correspondent.

"Famous and historical figures are one centering on God."
This is not a dispatch from the earth to the earth, but a special dispatch report from the heavenly world to the earthly world. This is the heavenly world, the world after death, where so-called souls live. I myself am deeply surprised at the phenomenon of being able to report from the world after death to the earthly world. Also, this Divine Principle lecture facility is filled with exclusive stories of such great significance that they are unprecedented in history. The Four Great Saints are here together, providing all the famous people in

history with Divine Principle education so as to establish a new view of God, of the universe and of human life. Through this program, all the famous historical figures are being united as one centering on God. How can such a thing be possible? On the earth, putting the idea of a universal community into practice is nothing more than a slogan. There is no instance in human history where it was actually accomplished. I hope people on earth will keep in mind that this is not something happening on earth, but in the world after death. Such a thing would be impossible in the earthly world.

Then who is the one who is behind all these phenomena in the spirit world? According to the people in charge here, his name is Sun Myung Moon and he is now on earth. I am told he is the True Parent and Savior of humankind who, after Jesus, has taken on the mission of Christ at the Second Advent and received the Divine Principle in a revelation from God. He has lived his entire life for the sake of peace among humanity, and he administers the heavenly and earthly worlds. Frankly, I, Peter Smark, find it almost impossible to understand this. What ability could a person on earth have that would allow him to administer what is happening in the heavenly world? Have you on earth heard of such things? I am certain that you will answer, No." That is my answer, too. According to the explanation by the sponsors, there is a specific period during which things in the heavenly world can be made known to people on earth, and people on earth can be told that the world after death definitely exists. They say this can happen only by the authority of the Messiah. I can neither affirm nor deny this. I can only conscientiouslly report that such things are happening in the heavenly world. Right now, there is a very sober atmosphere here. Everyone is being changed by the Divine Principle.

Peter Smark, 17 May 2002

11. **Jerzy Turowicz** 1912-1999. Died at age 86. Editor of the Polish Catholic weekly Tygodnik Powszechny. Decorated with the Commander's Cross with the Star of the Polonia Restituta Order. Received honorary degrees from Yale University and Boston University.

"The Divine Principle contains the pain and sorrow of history."

We are born with freedom of thought. So, in society, freedom of expression and freedom of the press are constitutionally protected. I, Jerzy Turowicz, have received a special opportunity to experience freedom of the press to its fullest extent here in the heavenly world, the world after death. This is an opportunity to send a message from the heavenly world to the earthly world. This is the greatest honor and joy. I met Dr. Sang Hun Lee here in the Divine Principle lecture facililty and received new wisdom concerning the Divine Principle. I would like to candidly report this to people on earth. Dr. Lee devoted his full sincerity and his heart and soul in lecturing to me.

The content was as follows:
a. Does God Exist?
b. Cosmology (The Principle of Creation)
c. The Path We All Must Tread (The Fall)
d. The Last Days And Our Attitude (Eschatology)
e. The Messiah We All Await:

Who Is He?
From Where And How Does He Come?

a. Resurrection (Will We Really Be Resurrected?)
b. What Is The Extent Of God's Predestination For Us? (The Human Portion of Responsibility and the Predestination of God's Will)
c. Is Jesus God Himself? (Christology)
d. Where Is History Headed? How Is It Getting There? (Principle of Restoration through Indemnity)
e. The Missions of Historical Central Figures (from Adam to Jesus)

f. Age of the Prolongation of the Providence of Restoration viewed in the Parallel Providential Periods

g. When And Where Will Jesus Come Again?

This is very wide-ranging content. For me, it was a time of tears. I regret that I cannot report everything here. People on earth, pay attention to this exclusive report from the heavenly world. This Divine Principle contains the bloodstained pain and sorrow of history. People on earth should not miss the opportunity to attend the Reverend Sun Myung Moon and study the Divine Principle. I went to the Divine Principle lecture facility in my capacity as a reporter, but I came to realize an incredible fact. I only regret that I can only convey it to people on earth in simplified form. I sincerely ask that you not miss that opportunity during your life on earth.

Jerzy Turowicz, 17 May 2002

12. **Shigeo Saito** Died 1999 at age 71. Reporter for Kyodo News Service and non-fiction writer. Recipient of the Japan Congress of Journalists Award.

"Reverend Sun Myung Moon deeply loves Japan."

I, Shigeo Saito, convey this message to the people of Japan. There is an eternal heavenly world for humankind. When I had a physical body, I was unconcerned and ignorant about this heavenly world, but it definitely exists Today, I would particularly like to convey to Japanese people that there is something Japan today seriously misunderstands and over which Japan is in serious error. I am now in the Divine Principle lecture facility. A great many people are changing here through the Divine Principle. This is a place where there is absolutely no religious or philosophical prejudice or racial discrimination. The heavenly world is creating the world of peace centering on this place. Japanese people here know the Divine Principle very well.

People here are aware that the Japanese media have for the past several years reported that the Divine Principle creates confusion in society. As I come to realize the true nature of the Divine Principle in the heavenly world, however, I must point out the bias and prejudice of the Japanese people.

Japanese people are mistaken about the Reverend Sun Myung Moon, who discovered the Divine Principle. He is living a life of total dedication to the purpose of leading all humanity on the right path. The Japanese people and government should correct their perception of this teacher and be guided by him. We Japanese should live our lives with a heart of atoning for our oppression of the Korean people, which is historical fact. Only then will Japan's future be certain. The Reverend Sun Myung Moon loves Japan deeply.

He loves our country with the heart of a father. I sincerely hope that Japan will never repeat its historical error toward the Korean people. For Japan to have a bright future, we must receive the guidance of the Reverend Sun Myung Moon. All the young people of Japan must receive the Reverend Moon's philosophical guidance. I strongly felt and realized this here in the spirit world. I sincerely urge that Japan not repeat its providential historical errors, and advise that it receive guidance from the teacher whom God has sent. This is because you must practice the teachings of the Divine Principle and Unification Thought in your daily life on earth if you are to live well here in the heavenly world. The world after death definitely exists.

Shigeo Saito, 17 May 2002

Messages of Peace from 36 Former American Presidents

God's Message to the United Nations

My beloved Children!

I am Jehovah, Lord of hosts.*
I am Jehovah, Lord of hosts.
I am Jehovah, Lord of hosts.

The endless, thorny path, a path of everlasting endurance and patience over the tens of thousands of years I have sought my beloved children has been a path of blood and tears that I, Jehovah, have shed.

I, Jehovah, Lord of hosts, am your parent, the father of all humanity. I am the parent of humanity, my children, my beloved children!

My dear children! I have cried out for you through endless nights for tens of thousands of years. I have yearned to call out your names and have called for you time and again. Yet, the words "dear children" have been ensnared for tens of thousands of years, so that even though I cried out for you, and my cries echoed around the world, you have been deaf to my calling. Can you understand even a little of this parent's heart, my heart, as I have has wandered around looking for my children?

My beloved children, my children participating in the United Nations! Even though your skin colors, characters, languages and cultures are different, in my eyes all of you are equally my children. All of you are beloved children of God; you are brothers and sisters who must love each other.

Imagine how I must have felt as I watched brothers and sisters live separated from each other, hating each other, fighting and killing each other with swords, guns, missiles and brute force. Now, I hope all of you will realize deep down in your hearts that each and every one of you are incarnations of me who are very precious to me.

My children! My beloved children! What would you do if you were to see a child of God, one of your brothers or sisters, dying of hunger? Can't you be done with the past, in which you have lived thoughtlessly, and think of me as your parent, believe in me and follow me? Can you imagine your Lord God's countless days filled with grief and sadness as I have waited for tens of thousands of years with endurance and patience?

United Nations! Wake up. Stand up! Now, you must hold hands and become leaders and fighters in establishing the Kingdom of God. Then wouldn't the people of the world, among whom a vast gap exists between rich and poor, become brothers and sisters who would help and support each other and share everything they have?

I am Jehovah, Lord of hosts.

I am Jehovah, Lord of hosts.

I am Jehovah, Lord of hosts.

I ask you, I plead with all my heart for you to find the right path and follow it before more of the spirits of my beloved children fall ill.

Participants in the United Nations! What would you do if the sound of your children's wailing and moaning from hell rang in your ears? I wouldn't mind going barefoot on a path that is tens of thousands of miles long if I could save my children. I would run down that path in one breath. I have been going down that path for the last tens of thousands of years.

I have been a God of grief, a God of sadness, a God of waiting and a God of pain and suffering. If all the days of the tens of thousands of years could be tied together with a single thread, it would be made of only blood and tears. Look at history to the present day. Look back at our history. How is it possible to express in words everything that has happened in history?

My children who are participating in the United Nations! The problems that are obstacles to attaining peace for all of humankind cannot be solved by force alone. That is completely impossible. I have specially sent Rev. Sun Myung Moon, my beloved son, and the True Parent, as the Messiah to all humanity, so believe in him and unite based on his teachings. If you do so, you will feel, deep down in your hearts, that I am your parent and your father even though you cannot see or touch me.

Listen to the inner voice in your heart. You will hear it echo, "God, my father, please be with me always!" I am asking all of you, my beloved children, with all my heart to shoulder the many problems in your nations and solve them. I ask you to bear in mind always that the people of the whole world are one big family of brothers and sisters. Reflect on my heart, the heart of a parent who has to teach his own children, "I am your father." Think deeply about it.

Jehovah, Lord of hosts*
Midnight, August 1, 2003

1) George Washington (1789-1797)
First President of the United States

I, George Washington, am deeply moved to learn through Mr. Sang Hun Lee the identity of Rev. Sun Myung Moon, learn about Rev. Moon's accomplishments and philosophy, and come to a realization that he has appeared as the Messiah. I was introduced to poignant content, including the course of Rev. Moon's turbulent life and suffering that led to his ascension to the position of the True Parent of humankind, his bloody battle with Satan to discover the Divine Principle, his providential victories, and the circumstances of God as he oversaw the historical time periods that existed in parallel from ages past. In particular, I came to the realization that the Messiah is giving unlimited love to the people of the United States, and is offering the most profound sincerity and dedication in order to guide humankind to the philosophy of peace. Yet the people of America are greatly lacking in sincerity and dedication in attending the Messiah. I realize that the American people are blessed by the mere fact that the Messiah is present on American soil. Yet, they appear unable to realize this deeply. I am deeply distressed over this.

The government and people of the United States should accept the philosophy and teachings of the Messiah. They must realize this is a blessing God has given to America. For what purpose did America become the strongest nation in the world? You should remember that when your ancestors founded America, they began by attending God, recognizing him as being the highest pinnacle. But what is your situation now? America must repent. Examine the direction in which you should be going, and the reality of where you are going. Will God guide you to the path of eternal blessing? Only if the people of America repent and receive guidance in the teachings of the Messiah will America become God's eternal Eden.

George Washington; June 9, 2002

2) John Adams (1797-1801)
Second President of the United States

I met a most precious person here in the world after death. That person is Mr. Sang Hun Lee, an invaluable person of noble character, who is worthy of great trust. When I first met this man, it was not through a motivation of faith. We were in a place piled with books, and each of us was looking for some books when we happened to bump into each other. This was the beginning of our relationship. He greeted me as we were arranging a large number of books. He said, "I am not in a hurry, so you can go ahead. He said he would take his time in arranging the books. I felt attracted to this gentle and humble man. In the process of our discussing a number of different subjects, I came to hear the Divine Principle and Unification Thought. Mr. Lee told me that his life had changed through numerous dimensions as he lived steeped in the teachings of Rev. Sun Myung Moon. He had left his position as a medical doctor and lived absorbed in the words of Rev. Moon and the Divine Principle before coming here. When America was founded, God was truly with us. This is quite apparent in the nation's founding spirit. Now, though, I begin to think that God may turn away from America. I hope that the people of America will quickly realize that they are committing a great error. As I learn the Divine Principle, Unification Thought, and the philosophy of peace of Rev. Sun Myung Moon here, my earnest hope is that America will return to the form of Eden, the Kingdom of Heaven on earth that God has desired to see. For this, it is necessary that the people of America follow the teachings of Rev. Moon. I earnestly hope that leaders in all aspects of American life will not waste a single day in accepting the global philosophy of Rev. Sun Myung Moon, and that God will not leave America.

John Adams; June 9, 2002

3) Thomas Jefferson (1797-1801)
Third President of the United States; Author of the Declaration of Independence

A great saint, the Messiah, has been born in the calm country of Korea, so I shall speak from my heart with the desire that the bright light from the East shine on all people. The founding spirit of America is second to that of no other country in the world. I take pride in that. Yet in this place, the world after death, I am quite envious of the people of Korea, a calm and quiet country. Where is there any peace or happiness for the people of America, vexed by philosophical and racial struggle, and by numerous incidents of terror? The Messiah, the True Parent of humankind, brings the philosophy of peace for the sake of the world. See what happens when the leaders of America accept these teachings. See what happens when America no longer seeks after only her pride as the strongest country externally but makes an unbiased examination of herself to see what she has done for peace in the world.

People of America, rise again. Return to the nation's founding spirit. Follow the teachings of Rev. Sun Myung Moon, the Messiah to all people, who has appeared in Korea. There is no inconsistency between our founding spirit and his teachings. Well-known presidents and kings from history are excited by the greatness of his philosophy of peace.

America, rise again. Make America the land of God's new truth and new hope. That is the mission America is called to fulfill in this age.

Thomas Jefferson; June 10, 2002

4) James Madison (1809-1817)
Fourth President of the United States; Father of the U.S. Constitution

"I earnestly hope America will not lose its status as an eternally powerful country."

I waited a long time for an opportunity for Madison's message to be conveyed to earth. I believe that since America's founding, many countries have recognized its position and self-respect as a rich and powerful country. Today, however, the people of America have almost forgotten America's founding, spirit. Was the

Constitution established just to maintain a single country? The Constitution must be obeyed for as long its people shall live. But when people leave their lives on earth, they must all come here, the spirit world, without exception, in accordance with the way of Heaven. So, even on earth, people must obey the way of Heaven. There is something that people must fulfill for the sake of their eternal lives in the spirit world. All the people of America must follow the teachings in the Unification Thought and Divine Principle of Rev. Sun Myung Moon, who is the returning Lord in this age and the Messiah. I earnestly hope that the people of America will be active participants in and cooperate with the unification movement, which deals with both heaven and earth, and carefully study the Divine Principle and Unification Thought so that America will not lose its status as an eternally powerful country. This is my final conclusion as one who has studied Divine Principle and Unification Thought several times here.

James Madison; June 8, 2002

5) James Monroe (1817-1825)
Fifth President of the United States

"Study the Divine Principle and Unification Thought diligently."

While people are living on earth, fame, power, and wealth probably seem very important. Most people have lived as if their earthly lives would last forever, and continue to live so now. I, James Monroe, have experienced a time of indescribable inspiration here. I have learned through a new expression of truth called Divine Principle that God is the parent of all of us, and that the Rev. Sun Myung Moon has appeared on earth as the Messiah after a history of restoration through indemnity involving many complicated circumstances, and is extending the hand of salvation to humanity. To realize that the Messiah is giving tremendous grace to people on earth makes me feel jealous toward them. From another viewpoint, I also cannot help feeling disappointed with them. People on earth seem to know almost nothing about life in the spirit world. It makes no difference whether one is the president of a country, a person of low birth, or a beggar. We are all God's children. What use is fame or power in a relationship between a parent and his children, and how can there be rich and poor people among brothers and sisters? Most people of America live comfortably, so they cannot experience the poverty and hunger of other people, and they most likely have not thought about life in the spirit world. You must study about your life in the afterlife, and take an interest in this. Study the Divine Principle and Unification Thought of Rev. Sun Myung Moon carefully. I request this earnestly as a person who was once responsible for the people of America and as one who has come here before you.

James Monroe; June 12, 2002

6) John Quincy Adams (1825-1829)
Sixth President of the United States; Son of President John Adams, the second President

"The American people must return to the founding spirit of America."

As one of those who have been responsible for the people of America, I would like to impress upon them that life on earth is very brief. It is an overly common phenomenon that people, during their lives on earth, are not concerned with their lives in the next world. It seems that there are not many people who truly understand that people were created to live on earth for just a fleeting moment and then come here, the spirit world, to live eternally. Compared to the eternal spirit world, life on earth is extremely short. During your lives on earth, you must thoroughly prepare yourselves to live eternally here in the spirit world. Fame, power and property must not be the standard of values for people living on earth. Fame during your life on earth will not bring you special treatment here. Your life here in the spirit world will be determined by your standard of values during your life on earth. I have a request to make to you who are on earth. I would like you to study about Rev. Sun Myung Moon, who is carrying out the Unification Movement on earth, and follow his teachings. If you study the Divine Principle carefully, you will come to a conclusion about how you must live your life. I make this request because I loved America as the person who was responsible for that nation. Her people must return to the founding spirit of America.

John Quincy Adams; June 13, 2002

7) **Andrew Jackson** (1829-1837)
Seventh President of the United States

I am convinced that Rev. Sun Myung Moon is a prophet, the Messiah, the returning Lord, and True Parent of humankind sent by God. His teachings, the Divine Principle and Unification Thought, and his accomplishments are sufficient proof of this. His teachings are the only path for humankind to follow in this age. Moreover, when I see how God has guided the history of the providence of restoration, I firmly believe that Rev. Moon is the Savior of all humankind who is leading the Completed Testament Era. I earnestly request that the people of America receive the thorough ideological guidance of Rev. Moon's truth and attend him. He is the true leader of all humankind. God is the True Parent of humankind, so all people are brothers and sisters. This is a universal truth of this age that will begin based on true families. The people of America will be able to have a vision for their nation's future only when they follow his teachings.

I have come to realize with certainty that a life of wealth and fame on earth is of no use in any place or in any situation here. You must consider what you would do if you were to come here now, rather than in the distant future. If I had taught people about the world where the soul lives while I was president, then I probably could have been treated as a president here as well. Through the Divine Principle, I have come to realize the greatness of Rev. Sun Myung Moon. I am deeply moved. I have repented and cried tears like a waterfall. I have also realized that I was an ignorant leader. I have bitterly repented for failing to awaken the American people to the reality of our eternal life. Even belatedly, I would like to convey this information to them. On several occasions God has appeared here as jubilant rays of light or as a dazzling rainbow. In these mysterious and emotional experiences, all of us were deeply moved by God and greeted him with applause. We repented of our past in tears and participated in the Divine Principle seminar.

People of America! Life on earth is a fleeting moment. I hope you will start now to prepare yourselves for life in the eternal world. Do not forget even for a second the fact that Rev. Sun Myung Moon is the Messiah, the True Parent and a true teacher for humankind, and follow his guidance faithfully.

Andrew Jackson; June 16, 2002

8) **Martin Van Buren** (1837-1841)
Eighth President of the United States

"People on earth must receive the Messiah's direct guidance."

I candidly accept that I failed to accomplish my responsibility as the father of the nation when I was on earth. I also confess that I did not even comprehend my own existence on earth. Until now I have lived here in the spirit world experiencing numerous mental struggles and much agony over these responsibilities. How could I have lived in such ignorance as to not realize that God's eternal aspect resides within human nature and that there exists another world that is vast and eternal? God, who is our parent and who wants to live together with us for eternity, has always existed and has constantly given us his silent instructions and guidance. Words cannot describe how ashamed I am or how much I reproach myself for completely neglecting this fact. I came to know these things for a certainty through the Divine Principle.

I want to be sure to take this opportunity to tell the people on earth one thing. That is that the spirit world where every person must live forever exists for a certainty. Those who do not prepare themselves on earth for life in this world are certain to face suffering and pain here. I hope that you will come here after having walked the correct path on earth. The quickest way to do so is to receive the instructions of the Messiah, who is on earth. The Messiah in this age is Rev. Sun Myung Moon. He was sent by God. Please never forget this point.

Martin Van Buren; June 17, 2002

9) **William Henry Harrison** (1841)
Ninth President of the United States; Died after one month in office

"Divine Principle taught me the true meaning and value of life and its direction."

Anyone who, within his lifetime, is able to know God and his ideal is the most fortunate of all people. Human beings should live their lives in a state of understanding the true value of life, but most people do not know this. I, Harrison, have deeply understood the true standard of value for life after having studied the Divine Principle in this place. The Divine Principle is a precious message to the people in this age that was revealed by Rev. Sun Myung Moon. He is the Messiah sent by God, the Savior, True Parent, and a great prophet for humanity.

He is the true son of God whom all humanity, not only Americans, must attend and follow. It would be impossible for me to explain all these things, and even if I did you would not understand. You should study the Divine Principle. If you do, you will come to realize clearly the fundamentals of life and the direction it must go. While you are on earth, prepare for the world where you must live for eternity. To do this, you must study the teachings of Rev. Sun Myung Moon, receive his instructions and inherit the lineage of God.

William Harrison; June 18, 2002

10) John Tyler (1841-1845)
Tenth President of the United States; Succeeded to the presidency upon the death of President Harrison

"Thank you for revealing Heaven's secrets."

It was intended that every aspect of human life on earth be directly related to God, but people have lived in ignorance of this fundamental truth. I have never denied God's existence, but the message that "God is the parent of humankind" is one that I truly had never even imagined. The instant that the Divine Principle lecturer spoke the words, "God is the parent of humankind," a dazzling ray of light shone into the lecture room from somewhere above. It calmed all of our hearts and fascinated us. We welcomed this with applause, yet at the same time we wept many tears.

God enveloped us in this resplendent light, and said in a loud voice, "I am the almighty Jehovah, God, and your parent." Then he said in a soft and clear but deeply sorrowful voice, "I am your parent."

After speaking these words he again moved around the lecture room in the ray of light, and then departed. Everyone in the lecture room felt reverence toward what had happened, and we spent a few moments in silent meditation. I am truly grateful to Rev. Sun Myung Moon on earth, the Messiah, Savior, and True Parent of humankind.

How hard you must have worked in order to reveal such amazing truths. True Parents, you have revealed the secrets of Heaven and the deep and difficult providence of suffering that was hidden behind a veil. Please lead not just the people of America but all humankind to the truth of the Divine Principle.

John Tyler; June 20, 2002

11) James Polk (1845-1849)
Eleventh President of the United States

"The True Parents of humankind have appeared and are guiding us."
In the course of a person's life, the time spent on earth is only a short moment. Yet when people are alive on earth, they think that their momentary earthly life will last forever. I attended the Divine Principle seminar here in the spirit world in a considerably good environment, being treated well in an atmosphere of piety. This is a place where only intellectuals and presidents, kings and others of considerable stature are present. Here I have received instruction in Divine Principle, Unification Thought, the life course of Rev. Sun Myung Moon, God's situation, as well as the creation of human beings, the fall and the providence of restoration.

People of America, do you think you know what kind of places heaven and hell are? As long as you are in your physical bodies, you most likely cannot even imagine. If there is one earnest message that I would give to the people on earth, it would be that Rev. Sun Myung Moon, who is on earth, is working based on the theme, "God is the parent of humankind," and that he is the Messiah, the True Parent of all humankind who has appeared to guide us. You must never forget this fact. You must carefully study the True Parents' philosophy and truth. These are the conclusions I have reached in the spirit world.

James Polk; June 25, 2002

12) Zachary Taylor (1849-1850)
Twelfth President of the United States

"We are all strongly resolved to be absolutely obedient to the teachings of the true teacher."
All of our desires, hopes, and joys are almost useless after we

have shed our physical bodies. The revelation that God our creator is the parent of humankind is an incredible event that is of greater value than the spiritual and physical worlds put together. I do not think there has ever been a more precious, magnificent, and shocking event in all of human history. I was once the president and leader of a great nation. But that has no meaning here. After losing my physical body, I thought deeply and wept many tears here while reflecting on the value of my brief earthly life.

Rev. Sun Myung Moon, as the Savior of humankind, the Messiah and True Parent has brought a new light of hope not only to the people of America but also to the entire human race. So let us all make a strong determination to live in absolute obedience to the teachings of the true teacher. I earnestly ask that the people of America follow the guidance of True Parents absolutely.

Zachary Taylor; July 31, 2002

13) Millard Fillmore (1850-1853)
Thirteenth President of the United States; Succeeded to the presidency upon the death of President Taylor

"Only the Divine Principle can preserve America's continued development."

Though my time is short, I am exceedingly grateful. I have waited a long time for an opportunity such as this. I, Millard Fillmore, as president of a nation and as a man with great love for the people of America, convey the following with a sincere heart.

Even here in the spirit world, I am respected and treated properly as a president of the United States. However, I must let you who are on earth know my very real pain that, from the aspect of the perfection of character, the position of president is not sufficient to receive the best treatment here. Before I encountered the Divine Principle, no one here referred to me by the title of President or acknowledged this title. Since my contact with the Divine Principle, though, I have been treated like a mid-level executive. But I am stricken with awe. Until now I lived without realizing that human beings possessed such nobility; I lived in a distant plane, not sensing the fundamental values of human life. But now that I understand the basic truths, I feel very apologetic toward the people of America. I realize acutely that I failed to lead them properly. It seems clear that no one can become a true human being without awakening to the truth.

First, I call out earnestly to the American people. How can I record all the inspirations, excitement, and regrets that I have experienced here? I can only summarize these as follows. The citizens of America must come to a clear understanding as to the identity of Rev. Sun Myung Moon, who is on earth, and, moreover, in America. Moreover, I urgently ask them to study his philosophy and truth in detail, and come to embody it themselves. I have confirmed here that God's fundamental thought, all his secrets and the origins of his creation of the universe are being revealed through the Divine Principle. I discovered that it is the Divine Principle that recognizes my position as president. America's future development depends on how you receive the Divine Principle. I clearly say to you from here in the spirit world that you must rely solely on the Divine Principle. I feel deeply that this is the wisest course, and I convey this to you with urgency.

Millard Fillmore; December 4, 2002

14) Franklin Pierce (1853-1857)
Fourteenth President of the United States

"With the Divine Principle, preserve America's position as a great nation at the center of the world."

I, Franklin Pierce, who led America as president, still feel love and heartfelt concern for this nation, even in the spirit world. I hope that America will remember her past, when she stood tall, and firmly maintain her position and pride as a central nation of the world. All human beings, no matter who they are, will one day come to reside in the eternal spirit world. Therefore, you should spend your transitory earthly life thinking of what the spirit world must be like. Here, I have thoroughly studied the Divine Principle and "Head Wing" Thought. Divine Principle is the teaching of Rev. Sun Myung Moon, who is on earth. The people of America must awaken to the truth of this teacher's "Head Wing" Thought. America now faces unprecedented confusion and difficulty. I hope that you will successfully overcome the crisis of this age. You must overcome it through a philosophy of reconciliation and harmony if you are to achieve peace. All humanity must actualize the truth of the Divine Principle brought by Rev. Moon. All of the world must live by a philosophy of peace, not force. America must thoroughly learn and be guided by Rev. Moon's teaching, which explains that war, conflict, and friction must be resolved by means of a philosophy of peace, so that America's position as a great nation at the center of the world may be preserved. You need to understand clearly the significance for America of the Divine Principle brought by Rev. Sun Myung Moon. This is the special message I wish to give you.

Franklin Pierce; December 6, 2002

15) **James Buchanan** (1857-1861)
Fifteenth President of the United States

"If not for the teachings of Rev. Sun Myung Moon, humanity would have no vision for the future."

After receiving the Divine Principle training, my heart is filled with such emotion that it is difficult to express in words. I feel unbounded gratitude and joy to have been born as a human being. The loneliness and grief that God experienced through the ages so pains my heart that I must clasp my chest. God has been in deep sorrow throughout the ages, but now the Divine Principle is bringing a bright future to humankind. I am overjoyed that I have been able to experience this valuable training here.

What is the Divine Principle? I understand what it means, and although I had the position of a president I feel such joy that I want to dance. The details of the Divine Principle cannot all be recorded on this page. In a word, it is "a gospel for the salvation of humankind." Everyone must live with the Divine Principle at the center of his or her life. Not only Americans but also all the people of the world must become one through the Divine Principle and Unification Thought. The one who discovered the Divine Principle is Rev. Sun Myung Moon. He is the Messiah and Savior of humanity. If it were not for his teachings and vision, the future of humanity could not be guaranteed at all. If humanity does not follow him, it will fall into great chaos. You must attend the Messiah while he is alive on earth, and become one with his teachings.

People of America! As this is an urgent request from one who was once president of the United States, please keep it in mind. God does not want America to resort to military force and fight wars. He desires that all humanity become one as brothers and sisters through a philosophy of peace. Rev. Sun Myung Moon holds an incredible key that will lead humanity into a world of peace. Please inscribe this in your memories.

James Buchanan; December 9, 2002

16) **Abraham Lincoln** (1861-1865)
Sixteenth President of the United States; Preserved the Union through victory in the Civil War, and issued the Proclamation of Emancipation

"People of America, I wish for you to constantly go the way of obedience, aligned with the teachings of True Parents."
Rev. Sun Myung Moon, Mansei!
Returning Lord and Messiah, Mansei!
True Parents of humanity, Mansei!
I, Abraham Lincoln, have experienced incredibly wondrous and exciting moments, but I am saddened that there is no communication, or crossing back and forth, between the earthly and spiritual worlds. Without doubt, Rev. Sun Myung Moon is the True Parent of humanity. He shows us how to love one another and brings us together as one, with no discrimination among religions or races. He is accomplishing feats on many levels that would be utterly impossible if it were not for True Parents' teachings. People of America, do you think you can bring peace through war and military force? God has appeared before humankind as our parent. While I was listening to the Divine Principle lectures, I had a vision. In this vision, all the souls in this place, including black people, yellow people, and white people, and including Christians, Buddhists, Confucianists, and Muslims, all came together and danced for joy. Then I saw a bright light, that is, the brilliant light of God, and in that instant, I, Abraham Lincoln, wanted to also jump in among them and begin to dance.

People of America, people of the world! Black people are children of God, as are white people. At some time, all of you will have to gather here in the spirit world and walk side by side and live together. I simply came here and experienced this fact before you.

I am making a request to the people of America because I love you with an earnest heart. Rev. Sun Myung Moon has appeared as the Messiah and the True Parent of humankind. I hope that you will attend the Messiah and constantly walk the path of obedience based on True Parents' teachings. War and military force will only serve to create another human hell. Is it not time for the earthly world to declare an end to hell? A philosophy of peace for humankind comes from the Messiah. The life that you now live in the earthly world is only a fleeting and incomplete life. If you are to live in the eternal world with eternal happiness, you must above all else awaken to the truth of the Divine Principle and Unification Thought. This is my solemn request.

Rev. Sun Myung Moon, I respect you. I thank you very much for all you have done. I will attend you resolutely as the Messiah and returning Lord, tear down the walls between races and religious groups, and participate actively in True Parents' Unification Movement.

Abraham Lincoln; December 9, 2002

17) Andrew Johnson (1865-1869)
Seventeenth President of the United States; Succeeded to the presidency after the assassination of President Lincoln

"May America's greatness be remembered forever."

I, Andrew Johnson, have determined that I will offer all of my life to the new truth of the Divine Principle. As a former leader of America, I now make an urgent call to its people from this place.

The youth of America today have lost a sense of direction in their lives. This does not apply to all young people, but a large majority of them have fallen into a pleasure-seeking lifestyle and do whatever they want. Young people themselves cannot be solely to blame for the errors in their thinking. They are lost because there is no fundamental alternative today that is capable of leading them.

I want to make a solemn request of them. Rev. Sun Myung Moon, who has revealed a new truth, is working day and night as the Savior of humankind to accomplish the task of human salvation. Through the Divine Principle, Rev. Moon reveals clearly and concretely such matters as the purpose of the creation of humankind and the universe, and the relationship between God and humankind. The only fundamental solution capable of bringing salvation to humankind is Rev. Moon's Divine Principle and philosophy of peace.

I make a solemn request that all young people in America receive the guidance of the Divine Principle and Rev. Moon's philosophy. Young people in America today have fallen into a very dangerous philosophical stream. Only Rev. Moon's teachings are capable of guiding us all to God's fundamental principles and the correct path for our lives. These teachings also instruct us on how to prepare for the eternal world, that is, our original homeland in the Kingdom of Heaven.

I have not been permitted sufficient time and space on this page to record all that I have experienced and learned here. I earnestly wish that people will forever remember the greatness of America.

Andrew Johnson; December 12 and 26, 2002

18) Ulysses Simpson Grant (1869-1877)
Eighteenth President of the United States; Commander of the Union forces during the final period of the Civil War

"If humanity wants an end to war, it must accept Rev. Sun Myung Moon's truth."

Tens of thousands of years have passed from the time that God created humankind, but until now we have lived without knowing the fact that God and humankind are in a relationship of parent and child. This must be the greatest tragedy in the history of humankind.

Through the Divine Principle training session here, I have for the first time come to a definite realization that it was an improper beginning to human history that has brought about endless conflict and war between peoples and nations, making it impossible to bring peace.

The Divine Principle explains the details of the creation, the fall, restoration, and other matters in a concrete manner. I think that Rev. Sun Myung Moon's Divine Principle is capable of bringing about a revolution within humankind, a revolution of character, and a revolution of consciousness.

There has been endless division, strife and war in human history. Innocent people have constantly suffered and been killed in such wars. Hell in the spirit world has come to be overflowing with people. Wars are the greatest cause of human unhappiness.

How can this problem be solved? Only Unification Thought, Rev. Sun Myung Moon's philosophy of peace, can bring a fundamental solution to this problem. Rev. Moon holds the key. Who is Rev. Sun Myung Moon? He is the Messiah, the True Parent of humankind. In religion, particularly in Christianity, this is called the Lord of the Second Advent. I, Ulysses Grant, am convinced that this is true.

If all people desire an end to war, then I ask that they accept the truth revealed by Rev. Sun Myung Moon. I regret very much that I am in the spirit world and therefore am unable to give you the physical confirmation that you need to accept this. But I ask that you believe these things and follow. The people of America must listen more carefully to the Divine Principle if they want their country to remain great eternally.

Ulysses Grant; December 14, 2002

19) Rutherford Birchard Hayes (1877-1881)
Nineteenth President of the United States

"I wish the Americans to become a people with a character capable of encompassing the world."

I, Rutherford Hayes, enjoyed tremendous power and honor while I held the office of the presidency during my life on earth. I lived as though that power and honor were eternal. Here in the spirit world, however, no one recognizes me for the fact that I was once president. At first, I felt a tremendous sense of despondence and unfairness that I could hardly endure. Through many long years, I shouted out in an effort to establish my position and to call attention to myself, but it was of no use.

Eventually, I was given a very inspiring opportunity, and through this I was able to realize many things about myself. I want to convey these things to people on earth.

I came to realize that human beings live in two worlds—that is, the visible physical world and the invisible spiritual world. I particularly realized many things concerning life in the spirit world. The high-level content of the Principle of Creation, the existence of God, the Providence of Restoration, and salvation through the Messiah were so mysterious.

What is this? It is a truth revealed by Rev. Sun Myung Moon. This truth could well be characterized as a true textbook of life. Through it I came to feel deeply the importance of the earthly life, and I also grasped many things about life in the spirit world. I realized that if people live incorrectly on earth, then they will not be able to avoid a path of suffering in the spirit world. I realized that if people commit errors on earth, then in the spirit world they suffer in hell, which is a place where there is no relationship with God.

People of the earth! People of America! I cannot record here everything that I have experienced. I can only say that the Divine Principle is a great truth and that it is unmistakable that Rev. Sun Myung Moon holds all the keys to human salvation and peace. So I want to clearly convey that you need to study the Divine Principle deeply and come to the same conviction. While you are on earth, you must prepare well for your eternal life in the spirit world. And you must abandon your self-conceit that America is the world's only great nation. I wish that the American people would become a people with the character capable of encompassing the world.

Rutherford Hayes; December 15, 2002

20) James Abram Garfield (March 4-September 19, 1881)
Twentieth President of the United States

"The Divine Principle is the fundamental truth that explains the mysteries of the universe and of life."

I have been one who believes that God is the creator and master of all that is in heaven and earth and is able to control all matters of nations, peoples, and the world with his divine authority. However, when I discovered that he is also our parent it gave me such surprise and awe that I do not know what to do. I feel a great sense of shame and injustice that when I was responsible for the nation I could not teach its many people about God correctly. I feel such pain over this.

Rev. Sun Myung Moon appears to have experienced some profound circumstances in the process of discovering the incredible secret of heaven that God is the parent of humankind.

After realizing that God is the parent of humankind, I was sitting, and feeling ecstatic about the Divine Principle, when suddenly some blinking lights approached me and covered my entire body. At that moment, I felt such tremendous joy that I cannot express it in words. I could not hear any sound. But I could feel within myself an inspiration that endlessly repeated the words "My Father, my Father, thank you." At that moment, I felt such joy that I felt like flying. I felt like a young boy. I had many other such experiences as well.

I send these words to you in the earnest hope that you will firmly grab hold of God, who really does exist. Each part of the content of the Divine Principle is a fundamental truth that explains the mysteries of life and the universe. As one who once was president of the United States, I want to convey a frank message to the American people. You must follow Rev. Sun Myung Moon, who has revealed the Divine Principle and Unification Thought. I hope that everyone will consider this most seriously.

James Garfield; December 18, 2002

21) Chester Alan Arthur (1881-1885)
Twenty-first President of the United States

"Establishing God's kingdom is the ultimate goal of humanity."

It is really heartrending to know the fact that human beings, who are the lords of all creation, have existed during the course of history without clear understanding, and have not been able to reach the level of the other things of creation. And it pains me even more to realize that the presidents have contributed almost nothing to God's dispensation, as he tried to restore humankind through indemnity by sending the central figures of the providence. The axiom "God is the parent of humankind" caused me to feel truly ashamed of myself. Now I have come to know with certainty God's will, God's current situation and the purpose and direction of history. For humankind, there can be no other objective in relation to a people or a nation, or other things to choose, except the establishment of God's kingdom. Establishing God's nation is the ultimate goal of humanity.

To establish God's nation, the first thing would be for us here in the spirit world to concentrate on leading the many people here to the right path; and the people on earth should align themselves with Rev. Sun Myung Moon, the representative of God and the True Parent, and participate actively in the movement to realize global peace. I hope, in particular, that the American people will take a leading role in teaching those on earth who still do not know the Divine Principle and God's will.

We must realize deep in our hearts and feel keenly through the Divine Principle and Rev. Moon's teachings that the kind of lives that we have led have been entirely improper. In history, has there ever been a greater truth to reform our awareness than the Divine Principle? If there has, can you name it? American people! It will be very difficult to save America with your present way of thinking.

The true teacher and leader of humanity is Rev. Sun Myung Moon. Hold on to him tightly and delve into his teachings. God has helped America in many ways to earn and maintain the reputation of being the greatest and most advanced nation in the world. I hope and pray that you will never slip out of God's outstretched hand of eternal love.

Chester Arthur; December 30, 2002

22) **Stephen Grover Cleveland** (1885-1889 and 1893-1897)
Twenty-second and Twenty-fourth President of the United States

I can't tell you how much I have waited for this moment. I truly believe that the only solution that can save America, which currently faces complex problems, is the philosophy and truth revealed by Rev. Sun Myung Moon, the Lord of the Second Advent, the True Parent. In other words, it is the Divine Principle and his philosophy of peace that can save America. Currently, America is in a state of total chaos in many different spheres. Nonetheless, America does not have an ideology that can resolve this chaos, and is unable to set clear goals for herself. If the American people unite as one, aligning with True Parents' teaching and truth, in the future America will be able to maintain her reputation of being the greatest economic power and a nation of moral force.

American people! I ask you this earnestly as the 22nd and the 24th president of the country. Please remember my plea and keep it deep in your hearts. In alignment with True Parents' philosophy and the Divine Principle, initiate a new movement of ethical reform across the entire nation. I ask you with all of my heart to believe in and follow Rev. Sun Myung Moon as the Messiah to all humankind. The spirit world truly exists. Follow Rev. Moon's guidance. I ask you once more from the bottom of my heart.

Grover Cleveland; July 7, 2003

23) **Benjamin Harrison** (1889-1893)
Twenty-third President of the United States

"The Divine Principle and the Unification Thought should be the guidelines of your everyday lives."

If I had led my beloved people of America with the great truth of the Messiah while I served as president, I would have been remembered forever in history. I feel very frustrated that it was not possible for me to do so because I lived at a different time.

At present, I would like to pass on to the American people Rev. Sun Myung Moon's teachings and doctrine from here in the spirit world. I have many regrets about not having been born at the right time and in the right environment to enjoy the privileges of this era. The spirit world is the place to which all people must come in the end, but most people do not seem to realize this. I am speaking to all of you living on earth, but in particular, I would like to pass on a new message to the American people. Being a citizen of the greatest economic power on earth is nothing to boast of here in the spirit world. Preparations for life in the spirit world, where the inner person must reside forever, must be completed on earth. Therefore, you must reflect on your lives on earth every day, and put them in order.

I cannot help but reproach myself for not being able to pass on to you how I feel clearly. You must make the Divine Principle and Unification Thought, which have come through the True Parent, Rev. Moon, who is on earth, the guidelines for your everyday lives. You must realize deep down that it is the only way for people to live. As the president of a nation, as a leader, as a person who came to the spirit world before you, and as a pioneer in life, I earnestly ask those of you on earth, and the American people in particular, to follow this path.

Benjamin Harrison; July 9, 2003

24) **William McKinley** (1897-1901)
Twenty-fifth President of the United States

"We should serve Rev. Sun Myung Moon as the representative of God on earth."

I lived on earth thinking that once I was done with my life on earth, shedding my physical body after death, nothing would remain or exist any more, but now that I am here in the spirit world, I am very ashamed of the old-fashioned way of thinking I had in the past. In particular, I am so sorry and ashamed of myself as the president of a nation, who is supposed to teach and guide his people.

How can I fully express in a few words new truths about God and humankind, such as the relationship between God and man, the value of life, the providence of the restoration of human beings and history, which started off by going in the wrong direction? I implore the people of America as their 25th president. I implore you, the people of America, to serve the True Parent, the Second Advent, Rev. Moon and study in great detail the Divine Principle and Unification Thought, which express the basic principles of life. True Parents' teachings are the most precious, the greatest truth in all of history. The American people of this era must put into practice and exercise True Parents' teachings of true love on earth before they come to the spirit world. You must learn from the true teacher as if your lives were at stake. Only if you do so will you be free of regret once you end up here in the spirit world. On earth you should serve Rev. Sun Myung Moon as the representative of God. This is what I ask of you from the bottom of my heart, as a person who has come here before you, on my honor as the president of a nation.

William McKinley; July 12, 2003

25) **Theodore Roosevelt** (1901-1909)
Twenty-sixth President of the United States

"Only when you realize the truth about God's work can you know the significance of peace for humanity."

I was very envious of the other former American presidents who reported before me, and I am very grateful and joyful to have an opportunity to also pass on my message to earth. On earth, I became the youngest president in American history, and so I had more progressive inclinations than the others. When I listened to lectures on Rev. Moon's Divine Principle and Unification Thought here in the spirit world, I was so moved that I feel an ever-growing urge to be resurrected on earth every day.

That is because American leaders of today look down on moral values, waste material resources of various kinds on unreasonable projects, provide a declining level of education in matters of morality and character and cannot come up with a clear solution to the chaos of this time. Rev. Moon's Divine Principle and Unification Thought are far superior to the doctrine that America is founded on. Consider the current situation of Israel. Are they serving Jesus Christ and closely following his teachings?

At present, great secrets of heaven are being revealed through the Divine Principle and the Unification Thought. Do you know that an eternal world where people live truly exists? It is a pity that the words I speak cannot fully express the strong emotions and admiration I feel for Rev. Sun Myung Moon's teachings. I am really very grateful to Rev. Moon. Even if he is not the Messiah or the Savior in religious terms, when we consider his doctrine, it is more than enough for us to acknowledge him as the leader of the world.

People of the United States! I implore you to serve the true teacher of humanity and to accept his theology so that you can remain forever as the people of the greatest nation in the world. Rev. Moon has the answers in many different dimensions regarding the establishment of an eternal world of peace. When I see his projects for realizing a world of peace, I cannot hold my head up, because as someone who received the Nobel Peace Prize, I am too ashamed. Only when the American people follow his teachings can America remain as a great nation of prosperity and peace in front of the world. And only when you properly realize, in this time, the truth about who God is can you know the significance of peace for humanity. This is the main point of my message that I want to convey to you from my heart.

Theodore Roosevelt; July 14, 2003

26) William Howard Taft (1909-1913)
Twenty-seventh President of the United States

"The Unification Principle is the new truth that can revolutionize the consciousness of today's youth."

People on earth, regardless of who they are, would like to leave their view of life and of the world for posterity. I was not free from this kind of desire while living on earth, but as I left my body, entered the eternal spirit world and directly experienced it, I came to understand how absurd I had been in my writings. There are no words that could explain how embarrassed and puzzled I felt in my heart. People on earth can never imagine how things are in the spirit world.

The most important thing people should know is that the spirit world exists as vividly as the physical world does. My authority and honor as the president of a nation didn't carry any significant meaning here. How can the people on earth understand with their limited way of thinking that we can send out messages from the spirit world to the physical world?

I was quite shocked to learn the fact that God is the parent of all mankind. I believe it is indeed a shocking issue for the entire human race of this age. Rev. Sun Myung Moon is the one who declared this truth to the entire world. Amazing and shocking facts don't just stop here.

There are books on Divine Principle and Unification Thought. Though there are billions of books on earth, can anyone really find a concrete solution to liberate humanity from suffering and misery in any one of them? Those of you living on earth must study the Divine Principle. It is the book that introduces the new truth discovered by Rev. Sun Myung Moon, a man who has gone through all manner of hardship and privation. The book explains the creation, the ideal world, the purpose of life, the fall of man, the beginning and the process of human history and God's sorrow. I feel sorry that I haven't been able to record all the things I wish I could tell you here.

I believe that the Divine Principle will completely revolutionize the fallen consciousness of today's young people. When I examine my own achievements as America's 27th president, I feel nothing but remorse and shame. I hope that people on earth will deeply study the reason God was revealed as the parent of all humanity in this age.

William Taft; July 16, 2003

27) **Thomas Woodrow Wilson** (1913-1921)
Twenty-eighth President of the United States; Advocated the establishment of the League of Nations

"Rev. Sun Myung Moon is the light of the human race and his teaching is the good news for us all."

Most people want to live healthier and longer on earth. However, when I came here to the spirit world, my earthly life felt just like a passing shower in the middle of a summer day. Although this brilliant and radiant life in the spirit world was waiting for me, during my earthly life I thought that life on earth was everything there was. I truly regret that my life on earth was false and in vain. Yet I came to understand that the physical life bore fruit in this eternal spirit world. I also came to understand that my position in the physical world as president of the United States didn't have anything to do with the kind of fruit I needed to bear in this world.

I deeply respect Rev. Sun Myung Moon. How could I respect someone whom I never met during my life on earth? Right here, I discovered his amazing truth. He had to go through enormous suffering to find the truth. Even now, in his old age, he works very hard to realize a world of peace. I don't think we can find a greater person than him in all of history. He is an absolutely unique individual in relation to bringing humankind into peace.

The Divine Principle testifies that Rev. Moon is the Lord of the Second Advent, Messiah, Savior and True Parent. I feel sorry that I cannot find still nobler names to call him. He is the light of all humanity, and his teaching is indeed good news for us all. People on earth may not feel that God is actually the parent of the entire human race, but the time will come soon when people experience the truth in concrete ways. The Divine Principle is something everybody must read. I highly recommend that not only Americans, but all the people of the world read this.

Thomas Woodrow Wilson; July 19, 2003

28) **Warren Gamaliel Harding** (1921-1923)
Twenty-ninth President of the United States

"If we practice the teaching of the Divine Principle, the whole human race can be united as one."

It was God's sorrow as well as a tragedy for the human race that the beginning of human history turned out badly and that God couldn't maintain his position as the parent of humanity. Reflecting on history, no one can deny that it has been full of misery due to such things as war, sickness and starvation.

I have come to understand Rev. Sun Myung Moon's idea of peace by participating in a Divine Principle seminar. After coming to know the true identity of Satan, I fell into a deep rage. How could this fact remain hidden as a secret throughout history? When I realized that sin, crime, war, disease, starvation and all human suffering were caused by our first ancestors' having gone astray from the path of true love, there were no words to explain the shock and surprise I felt. The entire human race must understand the teaching of the Divine Principle before tomorrow comes, reveal the true identity of Satan to all of heaven and earth and gain the wisdom necessary to liquidate all kinds of misery and disasters caused by Satan throughout history.

In short, God lost his position as our parent because of our ancestors. I can't simply explain all that here. Without the Divine Principle, there can be no true life. The Divine Principle is a guide to the basics of life. Many other presidents have already expressed their feelings. I agree with them absolutely. In order to pull out the root of fundamental human evil, we must reveal the true identity of Satan and his false love. At the same time, we must practice true love to change the way people reason and think.

We need to understand what kind of suffering and hardships Rev. Sun Myung Moon had to go through to discover the Divine Principle. If we all practice the teaching of the Divine Principle, the human race can be united as one, transcending racial, religious and national differences. There have been numerous teachings in history; yet only through the Divine Principle can humanity be led to the eternal world of peace. I sincerely pray that we, all humanity, serve Rev. Sun Myung Moon as our True Parent and practice the Divine Principle and Unification Thought so that we can live as one family of brothers and sisters.

Warren Gamaliel Harding; July 23, 2003

29) John Calvin Coolidge (1923-1929)
Thirtieth President of the United States

"God moves our original mind and is the embodiment of truth, beauty and goodness."

Many former U.S. presidents participated in a Divine Principle seminar and gave their impressions. I came to learn various new truths. I would like to mention one of them. America must realize that the entire human race is at a crossroads where it must make a decision and set off in a new direction. America is universally recognized as the most powerful nation on earth, but I see that America lacks the generosity and compassion to spiritually and materially give to other nations. The powerful can have true power only when they take care of the weaker. Because all people are brothers and sisters with a common parent, God, we must help, understand and depend on each other. That's God's long-standing wish. Even if we leave God out of the discussion, it is certain that man's original mind wants to live for the sake of others. Only then can people experience true joy and peace. Where does the activity of the original mind, which every person has, originate?

In the spirit world, I came to know many things by participating in the Divine Principle seminar. Most impressive was the teaching about the relationship between God and humankind. If each person did not have an original mind, this world would fall into utter confusion. The original being, the force leading the original mind, is God. God moves the original mind and is the embodiment of truth, beauty and goodness. He is also the parent of all humankind, so he guides people to lead a life of goodness. This is indeed an amazing fact.

Rev. Sun Myung Moon is the one who revealed this new truth. If America wants to keep its position as the most powerful nation on earth, she must accept this new truth and be willing to be guided by Rev. Moon.

John Coolidge; July 24, 2003

30) **Herbert Clark Hoover** (1929-1933)
Thirty-first President of the United States

"When there is harmonious interaction in every aspect of human society, all suffering and misery will disappear."

I am intimately grateful to those who convinced me to participate in the Divine Principle seminar. The Divine Principle applies universally, not only in the physical world but also in the spirit world, without any exception. Even so, we almost never realized that fact while living on earth. I can say that this is a viewpoint the many presidents participating in this seminar shared. What I was deeply impressed with was the Divine Principle topic on dual characteristics and relationships.

Complex problems in various aspects of human life with respect to the individual, family, nation and world come about because there is no harmonious interaction between different parties. If interaction is smooth on the various levels of life, there will not be any struggle, conflict or trouble in the life of an individual, or in a family or society. Furthermore, there will be no conflict or war between nations. That's the original way of life. When we understand the Divine Principle, all of this comes to us so clearly and simply. However, as individuals, we all struggle. The original God-centered mind and the self-centered mind struggle against each other. The mind and body struggle against each other as well. Therefore, when the mind and body become one centering on the God-centered mind, a person can be in control of him- or herself. Nevertheless, interaction has been cut off, distorted and abandoned in the most fundamental relationship in the cosmos— the relationship between God and man.

On earth, we have never clearly understood the fundamental truth that all things in the physical world and the spirit world exist in pairs (e.g. male and female). There is nothing in the world that doesn't exist in partnership with something of an opposite nature. God exists as a unified being of dual characteristics. In addition, the Divine Principle reveals with clear logic the purpose of life, the fall of man and the course of the restoration of humankind. The Divine Principle is the new truth of this age. The Divine Principle, which was discovered by Rev. Sun Myung Moon, is a unique guide to realizing world peace. The Divine Principle reveals that Rev. Moon is, according to the Christian expression, the Savior, the Messiah, the Lord of the Second Advent—and the True Parent of all humanity. I am incapable of describing all of Rev. Moon's achievements and ideas related to world peace, but I certainly have faith in him.

I would like to sincerely speak to all people on earth from here. All of you must actively be involved and interested in Rev. Sun Myung Moon and his teachings. If God is the parent of all people, we are brothers and sisters to one another. Yet humankind has lost its one center (True Parents), is in conflict and struggle, and people are fighting wars against one another. I absolutely respect and believe in Rev. Sun Myung Moon, who, as God's representative, is trying to bring all humankind to the point of being brothers and sisters under one parent, God.

Herbert Hoover; July 26, 2003

31) **Franklin Delano Roosevelt** (1933-1945)
Thirty-second President of the United States; Served four terms as president; Promoted the New Deal Policy in an attempt to solve the Great Depression of the 1930s

Franklin Delano Roosevelt's Prayer
Heavenly Father!

I think I am too bold to call you Father. Dear Father, you are so miserable! You are a God of great grief and bitter pain. What can I say to bring you words of comfort, Father? I am Roosevelt. At one time, as the president of the United States, I invested all my energy for the welfare and prosperity of the American people, but I didn't guide them in any way to help them prepare for life in the eternal spiritual world. It is this point that has caused my heart to feel untold suffering. Heavenly Father, please forgive me.

And dear God, please lead the American people today to the right path. Most of them are caught up with excessive self-praise and egoism just because they are citizens of the strongest power on earth. They are unable to display tolerance and humility toward the third world countries, they take their own future lightly, their own view of God is deviating from the true path.

Heavenly Father, please shake and wake up America. I pray earnestly for our American people. Heavenly Father, I beg for forgiveness that I was unable to teach them that you are the parent of all humankind. Heavenly Father, I will invest all my energy and prayers here in the spirit world until the day when all the American people become God's true children.

The new truth of the Divine Principle is moving my heart deeply, and is making me repent about everything in my past life. It is the first time in my life that I have had such deep feelings. I realized so many things through the Divine Principle, and the only thing that I can do at this time is lament loudly with tears of repentance.

Heavenly Father, please protect and preserve the throne of the True Parents, Rev. Sun Myung Moon who worked so hard to find and reveal this new truth. Father, I know that this prayer is presumptuous and impolite, but unless I pray and repent in this way before you, I will not be able to endure. I want to offer this prayer to you, dear God. Please accept it.

God's child, Franklin Roosevelt; July 26, 2003

32) **Harry Truman** (1945-1953)
Thirty-third President of the United States

"God is my parent, I am God's child." This is my favorite motto.

As one in a line of successive American presidents, I want to declare from the spirit world a shocking truth before not only the American people, but also the whole of humankind, including all those connected to the United Nations. It is the amazing fact that "God is the parent of humankind." Until today, all humankind has not been able to become one, and people are still suffering from war, disease and poverty. The advanced nations have too many resources, while the people of the third world are dying of starvation. In the Divine Principle, I discovered the fundamental solution to the problems of war, disease, and poverty, the disparity between the rich and poor, and the problem of human rights.

Why did the suffering and unhappiness of human beings begin? It was because the start of human history was wrong, because their master and center changed. The fact that human history is a false history might sound strange to those who are not interested in the view of Christian history according to God's providence.

What sort of existence is God in relation to humankind? God was the parent of humankind from the very beginning. But after God created Adam and Eve, it was the Archangel Lucifer who took care of them. However, the archangel Lucifer tempted them and established an immoral relationship of love with Eve while she was in the period of growth. He acted as though he were their master and parent and he came to control this earth. Unfortunately, human history started from this immoral, sinful blood lineage. This sinful blood lineage has been passed down from generation to generation throughout human history. And the result of this was that human society became an unprincipled society that God never wanted. From the very beginning, humankind lost the ideal world of God's creation which was to center on God's love. People lost their own humanity. The archangel Lucifer disguised himself as God, and has been controlling human history until today. Accordingly, human society is full of all kinds of sin and evil, and things reached such a state that materialistic communism even declared that there was no God. The original world of peace and love that God had intended has become a world where sin and evil are rampant. It is an unprincipled world with unceasing poverty, disease, conflict, struggle and war. This is the reality of the world today.

Today, humankind must clear up this unfortunate history and live together as brothers and sisters attending God as their parent. When this happens, then for the first time humankind will be able to be freed from disease, struggle, war and so on. This is the kind of world that God had planned at the beginning of creation.

It took a long time for me to realize this fact. I cannot emphasize enough the truth and greatness of Rev. Moon's Divine Principle. The Divine Principle contains God's ideal of creation and the blueprint for a world of peace. In short, the Divine Principle is the unique truth of humankind. It is the guidebook for a true life. The more you research the Divine Principle, the more you come to feel new life and new inspiration. Today, the final goal of humankind is to reveal day by day more about Satan's evil and to completely clear up the inheritance of sin and evil. When this is done, then for the first time a world of peace will be built centered on God's true love. And an ideal world of the Garden of Eden where all people live as brothers and sisters will be able to be realized.

People of the world! Brothers and sisters! Let us, centering on our True Parents, take part in the Unification Movement, spreading it to the whole cosmos. Let all humankind attend Rev. Sun Myung Moon as our True Parent and let us become the central people to build a world without poverty, or war and the like. Let us work to build the Kingdom of Heaven, the eternal world of peace, freedom and love. Then God's glory will become even more visible. The American people in particular should try harder than any other nation to comfort God's heart when he looks at all his children suffering in sin and evil.

"God is our parent, we are God's children." I want to suggest to all humankind that we take this to be our motto. This is both God's hope and our hope. I sincerely hope that the intelligentsia will not be lazy in studying the Divine Principle.

Harry Truman; July 28, 2003

33) Dwight David Eisenhower (1953-1961)
Thirty-fourth President of the United States

A letter to True Parents

Most respected True Parents, I am Eisenhower.

True Parents, you love humankind so much! I realized many things after I learned that even in your aging body you endure all kinds of suffering and adversity for the peace of humankind. In this place here, centering on Sang Hun Lee, all the American presidents have determined in their minds to guard and protect America today.

Life on earth appears like that of the satanic city of Sodom. As time passes, even though there is change, no one is clearly aware of what is wrong. And I know that there is no difference between God's heart and the heart of True Parents when they look at the lives of people living on the earth. When I see the faces of True Parents, who are always taking great pains to re-establish the Garden of Eden of God's ideal at the time of creation, I feel so ashamed.

There are still many things in True Parents' plan that are left to be realized and we are all doing our best to help you in the physical world. True Parents, please make the foundation for us so that we can resurrect on the earth to help your work! We all deeply realize that without True Parents' Divine Principle and Unification Thought there would be no future for the world. Please allow us a foundation where we can work, receiving your orders.

Today, the United Nations and America are confronted with the situation where they absolutely need the ideology of the True Parents. Let the American people take part in the movement to realize world peace and lead all humankind so that they can become one through the ideology of the True Parents. Every time God sees his true son fighting alone, his distressed face is covered by dark clouds of worry. I really feel such sorrow. Now, even if it is in this place, the presidents of the United States are resolved, centering on the ideology of True Parents, to actively take part in the movement for the settlement of world peace. If you look at our solemn and resolved faces you will receive comfort. Please forgive me for daring to write this letter to you.

Dwight Eisenhower; July 29, 2003

John Fitzgerald Kennedy (1961-1963)
Thirty-fifth President of the United States

A Message to the United Nations

Those of you at the United Nations, I am John Kennedy!

I want to declare an extremely important thing to you today. The fact that Kennedy is sending a message from the spiritual world to the United Nations is something that cannot be imagined in your world, and it is very significant news. Through attending lectures of the new truth, Divine Principle and Unification Thought here in the spirit world, I have understood the direction and goal that the world must take today. I want to let the UN know the following.

The people of the world today must live as brothers and sisters, helping and depending upon each other. This is the most urgent and universal value. I want to convey to those of you at the UN this strong message showing our resolution and will, hoping that you will put it into practice. I declare the following:

1. God is the parent of humankind and truly does exist.
2. After people finish their life on earth, their soul continues on to live in the eternal world, namely the incorporeal world (spirit world) which is a reality.
3. Rev. Sun Myung Moon is the Messiah, the Savior and the True Parent of humankind.
4. All of humankind and the UN have to understand the ideology and works of Rev. Sun Myung Moon and they have to accept his leadership and guidance.
5. The realization of an eternal world of peace is only possible

when we put into practice the ideology of the True Parents and practice love on the supra-religious, supra-national, and supra-racial levels. A world of peace cannot be realized through wars or through force.

6. The whole of creation, including humankind, exists in reciprocal relationships, namely, both internal nature and external form, and plus and minus (male and female).
7. The beginning of human history went wrong and this has to be restored according to the providence of restoration.
8. We have to clearly know the true identity of Satan (Lucifer) who left a huge stain on the beginning of human history.
9. The gap between the rich and poor is becoming more serious on the earth. The cause of ignorance, sickness, poverty and war has to be completely eradicated.
10. The Divine Principle and Unification Thought are the unique textbooks that can free humankind from suffering and unhappiness.

I sincerely hope that those of you at the UN keep these ten points in mind and in your own countries fulfill your responsibility in this age to lead humankind into a new future. Members of the United Nations, don't ask what the United Nations can do for you, ask what you can do for the realization of the eternal world of peace (the original founding purpose of the UN). I feel sorry to God that during my short term as president the UN did not fulfill its responsibility and, with a heart asking for forgiveness, I send this message.

John Kennedy; July 30, 2003

35) Lyndon Baines Johnson (1963-1969)
Thirty-sixth President of the United States

Who is God?

Each person among us has the desire to seek out goodness. Whether or not people believe in God, when they face difficulties, even though they may not recognize it by themselves, they are looking for some being who can help them. What being is that? I think the being that is the origin of that desire to seek and find— a desire that is settled deep within the original mind—is none other than God.

People of America! I have directly experienced God in the spirit world. One day, a brilliant light of unknown source surrounded me and I was whisked off to a very miserable place. In that place I could hear strange groaning noises and screams. And I myself involuntarily shouted out, "Help me, save me!"

At that time, the light began to swirl around my chest and a voice said, "Save America! Save humankind! Proclaim the existence of God! I am Jehovah, Lord of hosts * I am Jehovah, Lord of hosts * I am Jehovah, Lord of hosts *! I am asking you to save America, and thus to save the world." In that one moment, I was both enraptured and fearful. I felt that this place was hell, and the miserable people there were experiencing the manifestation of the fruits of their earthly lives.

My fellow Americans! What kind of being do you think God is? He is the creator of heaven and earth, and of humankind. Rev. Moon's Divine Principle clarifies that God is the parent of humankind. This discovery is a remarkable one. God definitely exists, and mostly appears to people in the form of light. If you receive the Divine Principle and the guidance of Rev. Sun Myung Moon, you will work this out in detail. Please put your brief earthly lives in order and prepare yourselves properly so that you can settle in a place full of light in the eternal spirit world. This is my desperate plea.

Lyndon Johnson; July 31, 2003

36) **Richard Nixon** (1969-1974)
Thirty-seventh President of the United States

Proclamation of Resolution of Former US Presidents

MC: Dwight Eisenhower
Prayer: Franklin Roosevelt
Adoption and Proclamation of Resolution:
Richard Nixon
Three Cheers of Mansei: Richard Nixon

Prayer
God our Father,
We, the former presidents of the United States, in the attendance and service of God and True Parents, hereby proclaim our adoption of the following 6-point written resolution. We all determine to actively volunteer our efforts and sacrifice for the sake of peace in the United States and peace for all humankind. For this we ask that you guide us all.

Proclamation of Resolution

1. We proclaim that God exists as the parent of humankind.

2. We resolve and proclaim the reality of the incorporeal world (the eternal spiritual world).

3. We resolve and proclaim that Rev. Sun Myung Moon is the Lord of the Second Advent, the Messiah, the Savior and the True Parent.

4. We resolve and proclaim that we will make public to the whole world the true nature of the devil, Satan (Lucifer), who destroyed the original culture of humankind, and that we will eradicate the root of the various sins that have manifested throughout history.

5. Affirming that world peace can never be realized through military strife or war, we resolve and proclaim that we will realize world peace based on the true love of True Parents.

6. We former US presidents resolve and proclaim that we will stand in the forefront with the heart to volunteer and sacrifice for the sake of world peace.

Three Cheers of Mansei
Hananim (God), Mansei!
Champumonim (True Parents), Mansei!
Former US Presidents, Mansei!

Former US Presidents Representative Richard Nixon
July 31, 2003